DISCIPLESHIP EXPLORED

LEADER'S GUIDE

For the Universal Edition and International Student Edition

Discipleship Explored: Universal Edition Leader's Guide

www.christianityexplored.org

Published by
The Good Book Company
Tel (UK): 0845 225 0880
Tel (int) + (44) 208 942 0880
Email: admin@thegoodbook.co.uk

Websites
UK & Europe: www.thegoodbook.co.uk
N America: www.thegoodbook.com
Australia: www.thegoodbook.com.au
New Zealand: www.thegoodbook.co.nz

ISBN: 9781906334857

Grateful thanks to: Paul Chelson, Barry Cooper, Steve Devane, Kerry Fee, Alison Mitchell, Andre Parker, Sam Shammas, Tim Thornborough, Nicole Wagner Carter and Anne Woodcock, and the many others who contributed to the development of the *Discipleship Explored Universal Edition and International Student Edition*.

BRITISH LIBRARY CATALOGUING IN PUBLICATION DATA. A catalogue record for this book is available from the British Library.

Design by The Good Book Company

Printed in China

Introduction

Welcome to the Universal Edition of *Discipleship Explored.*

This eight-week course is designed as a follow on course to *Christianity Explored,* in which people are introduced to the basics of the Christian faith through reading and discussing Mark's Gospel. The course aims to take people the next step in their understanding of what it means to follow Jesus Christ – that is to be his disciple.

Discipleship Explored is different from many basic courses for new Christians. They are often concerned to put in place some of the mechanics of following Christ: prayer, Bible reading, church membership etc. But this course is built around a detailed study of Paul's letter to the Philippians – a group of believers who had recently started out on the Christian life.

During this eight-week course, your group will work their way through this short letter learning from the example of these early believers, and the teaching that they were given. What your group will learn is so much more than a simplified 'how to' of the Christian life. They will discover the inevitability of suffering for our faith; they will see the need to guard the truth against false teachers; they will learn the need for personal holiness as they hold out the word of life to others; and they will find out the secret of true contentment.

CRYSTAL CLEAR LANGUAGE

This Universal Edition is written with a concern to make the language crystal clear and accessible to the widest range of potential users throughout the world. Many of the words in the Bible are complex and difficult to understand for those who have been believers a long time, let alone those who are just taking their first tentative steps. So these studies are designed to be suitable for a wide variety of groups, including those for whom English is a second language.

Those starting this course, perhaps after having finished *Christianity Explored,* may have already made a commitment to Christ, but many will not. It is our prayer that, as people discover the challenge, joy, fellowship and contentment that comes from knowing Christ and following him, they too will come to trust him as their saviour as they meet with you week by week.

This Leader's Guide is divided into two sections. The first will train you to use the course, and the second will be your guide each week as you lead the studies, giving answers, background and other helpful information to encourage you as you lead your group through Philippians.

Contents

SECTION 1: HOW TO RUN THE COURSE

Planning your Discipleship Explored group 9

Preparing yourself and your co-leaders 13

Introducing Philippians 17

Running the sessions 19

What to do if... 23

Working with English speakers 27

Cross-cultural discipleship 29

You never stop learning to be a disciple 35

SECTION 2: STUDY GUIDE

Before We Begin 41

WEEK 1 **How can I be sure I'm a Christian?** *Philippians 1:1-11* 43

WEEK 2 **What am I living for?** *Philippians 1:12-26* 51

WEEK 3 **Together for Christ?** *Philippians 1:27 – 2:11* 59

WEEK 4 **How should I live for Christ?** *Philippians 2:5-18* 67

WEEK 5 **Can I be good enough for God?** *Philippians 3:1-9* 75

WEEK 6 **How can I know Christ better?** *Philippians 3:10 – 4:1* 83

WEEK 7 **How can I rejoice in Christ?** *Philippians 4:2-9* 91

WEEK 8 **How can I be content in Christ?** *Philippians 4:10-23* 99

EXTRA **An example to follow?** *Philippians 2:19-30* 107

SECTION 1

How to run the course

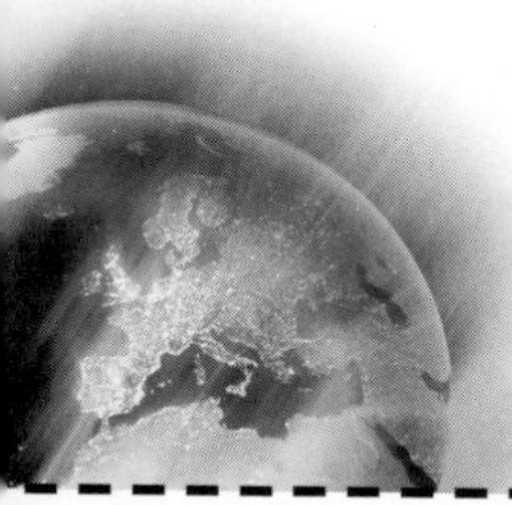

BEFORE THE COURSE

Planning your Discipleship Explored group

Helping a new believer on their first steps in the Christian life has to be one of the most exciting and rewarding experiences available to us. It's also vitally important – because the patterns of thinking, belief and behaviour we encourage in them will set an important pattern for the rest of their lives. We have an opportunity, with God's help, to help a new Christian build a life of joyful and effective service.

You may be someone who usually skips introductions, but can we please encourage you to read through these notes carefully. They will help you prepare properly for your important role as a spiritual guide and friend.

WHO WILL COME?

Discipleship Explored is a course that explores what it means to follow Jesus, and is written for those who are new Christians. However, there will be many who will benefit from this course who do not fit into this category. You may have:

- **People who are not yet Christians.** *Discipleship Explored* is a follow-on course to *Christianity Explored.* Many who finish that course will still be at the investigating stage, and may not yet have made a clear commitment to Christ. Do not be concerned about this. During the course they will have the facts of the gospel repeated to them, and they will discover more of the reality of what it means to be a follower of Jesus.

- **People who are unsure if they are Christians.** For many people, the experience of coming to Christ is a long drawn-out process, with several important moments of decision and understanding along the way.

- **People who have been Christians for a while.** *Discipleship Explored* is a terrific refresher course in what it means to be a follower of Jesus, and will help people grow who may have been Christians for years.

Because the course involves discussion, it is best to limit the size of a group to a maximum of 12 (6-8 if you are working with internationals). More than this, and the quieter people in the group will not feel able to participate. It may be best to have separate groups for those with English as a second language, as this will allow everyone to go at a pace they are comfortable with – but don't worry if this is not possible.

HOW WILL I INVITE THEM?

Advertise the course in your church bulletin, during the Sunday services and at events you run for internationals. Explain who the course is for, and what will happen at it.

At the end of *Christianity Explored*, participants should be invited to join *Discipleship Explored*. The *Christianity Explored* leaders will know who from their group is ready to go on to *Discipleship Explored* and should be encouraging them to do so.

The beauty of studying Mark's Gospel in *Christianity Explored* is that participants should now be eager to explore another part of God's word. Not only that, but they will also want to maintain the friendships they have developed while on the course.

You can make your own invitations and posters using the downloadable logos available at www.discipleshipexplored.org. You might also use the *Discipleship Explored* trailer from the DVD, also downloadable from the same website.

WHERE WILL WE MEET?

Try to find a place where you will be able to meet every week at the same time. The important thing is that the environment should help people relax so that they will be encouraged to discuss freely. Sharing a meal together will help with this.

Comfortable church premises provide a neutral meeting ground that is also free of distraction.

Homes are another option, but be aware that some may not be used to visiting one another's homes. Alternatively, some groups may meet in a hired room. Be careful of choosing a place that is too exposed to the public, where there can be many distractions or people may feel embarrassed.

If your group has previously done *Christianity Explored*, then it's ideal if you can continue to meet in the same place.

WHEN WILL WE MEET?

Once a week for eight to ten weeks is the time required to complete the course. You should be able to complete the studies in $1\frac{1}{2}$ to 2 hours, depending on the ability of the group.

Choose the time to suit the particular group of people you are aiming at. Often Christians can get into a rut when planning meetings. We may have become used to meetings that start at 7.30pm and end by 9.30pm. That may or may not be the best time for the guests. Have you considered that lunchtime may be best for some kinds of groups, or even early morning, mid morning or afternoon? Be imaginative, but realistic, about the people being invited, and ask them what might suit them best.

You will also need to spend time with the participants outside of the course in order to have the time to deal effectively with issues that come up during the studies. Time spent with individuals is also the quickest way to develop a trusting relationship.

A caution: it is completely inappropriate to be meeting up one-to-one with members of the opposite sex. There may also be important cultural differences that you are unaware of if you are meeting with someone from another country. See the section on Cross Cultural Discipleship on page 31 for more about this.

WHO WILL LEAD?

Ideally, you should have two leaders for every six participants. The leaders are responsible for guiding the studies and discussion. In a mixed group, it is desirable to have both a male and a female leader so that they can deal with pastoral situations appropriately.

Leaders should be Christians who are able to teach, encourage discussion and care for participants. They should be able to teach the Bible faithfully and clearly, and handle pastoral situations with care and sensitivity.

WHAT WILL WE NEED?

- **Food.** If you are able to share a meal together, it will make the whole experience better. On a practical level, people will talk and participate more if they spend more time together, and they will open up to you as the leader more as they spend more time with you. If it is impractical to serve a meal, provide light refreshments (coffee and cake, for example). Getting your group members involved in bringing food, or helping in its preparation, will help them feel it is 'their group' rather than something that you are running for them.
- **Bibles.** Everyone on the course – leaders and participants – will need a Bible. There are downloadable sheets of the Philippians material in the NIV version available at www.discipleshipexplored.org, or you can download and print out other versions of the Bible, including foreign language versions, from www.biblegateway.com

  For the sake of clarity, it is important that everyone uses the same version. (The version used throughout the course material is the New International Version.) If they do not already have one, participants should be given a Bible at the start of the course, preferably one they can take away with them. In many cases it will also be essential to provide participants with a copy of the Bible

in their own language. You can find information on locating Bibles at www.
discipleshipexplored.org.

- **Study Guide.** Make sure you have enough copies of the Study Guide so that every participant has their own copy. Provide pens as well.
- **DVD.** It is not essential to use the DVD for the Universal edition of *Discipleship Explored,* but you may find it useful to show it as a kind of summary at the end of the study. Certainly, watching the programmes yourself will increase your understanding of Philippians, and help you to explain it more clearly to your group.

BEFORE THE COURSE

Preparing yourself and your co-leaders

YOUR OWN CHRISTIAN LIFE

We want to help new Christians to grow in spiritual maturity, equipping them to serve God faithfully wherever they are. We want them to learn to obey Christ as Lord – that is what it means to be a disciple.

One thing we will discover in Philippians is the importance of the personal example and godliness of a leader. People learn about what it means to be a disciple, not just from the things we teach, but from our behaviour as well.

That's why Paul tells Timothy to "set an example for the believers in speech, in life, in love, in faith and in purity ... watch your life and doctrine closely" (1 Timothy 4:12, 16).

Read the following verses and then write down what it will mean for you to "set an example" during *Discipleship Explored.*

- **John 13:35**
- **Romans 15:14**
- **Ephesians 4:29**
- **Ephesians 6:18**
- **Hebrews 10:24**
- **1 Peter 3:8-9**

Pray that you would be able to put these verses into practice.

YOUR UNDERSTANDING OF THE BIBLE

- **Get to grips with Philippians.** You will need to be thoroughly familiar with this letter. Although it is short, it involves complex ideas that can be hard to understand. Work through the introduction to Philippians on page 4 of the Study Guide, but also read the letter several times. A good commentary would be helpful (see page 18 for recommended commentaries). We have supplied some material to help you in the second section of this Leader's Guide, but there is more you should be getting to grips with.
- **Think about the passage from your group member's point of view.** What might they not understand? What questions and problems might come to their minds? Which words will you have to explain to people learning English? (There is a words list to help you each week.)
- **Think about different ways of explaining things.** Although this is a Bible study, some people think visually, so you might want to get a whiteboard or a large sheet of paper to write on. This is also useful for writing up new words (for those learning English). You may be able to think of some diagrams / illustrations which will help people to understand an important point.

YOUR KNOWLEDGE OF THE MATERIAL

- **Know the material.** Go through the questions in the Study Guide, watch the DVD and read the notes in this Leader's Guide – so that you know where the session is heading, and can guide the group through it.
- **Make the material yours.** In any course, you will need to do some adaptation to suit your particular group and circumstances. We have put a large amount of thought, experience and testing into developing this course. If it is in here, it is in for a good reason. But you will need to think up some illustrations, stories, analogies, personal experiences etc that you might want to use, so that it is personalised for you.
- **Work out how long things will take.** You will need to know the material well enough to know how to speed up or allow longer on the various questions. Don't rush – give people time to digest what the Bible is saying and its implications, and remember that those with English as a second language will need more time to think than native speakers. But don't let it drag on, especially if the discussion is going off the subject. Work out (and write down in your booklet) approximately how long each section should take. *Remember, it's best to finish with people wanting more, rather than feeling that the session went on forever.*
- **Plan time to prepare.** Putting the dates of the meetings in your diary is not enough. Plan time for preparation, administration, arriving early to set up, and time to meet up with group members outside the meetings. And of course, time to pray...

YOUR PRAYER COMMITMENT

One of the main reasons why we don't pray is that we don't plan to pray. As you set aside time to prepare for your *Discipleship Explored* group, include time for praying for the other leaders, hosts and guests.

- If you are a lone leader – then ask someone else to pray with you each week.
- If there are a number of leaders – then meet up and pray.
- Why not organise a prayer group? – recruit people from your church to pray for you as you meet together with your guests for each session.
- And remember to pray yourself – keep a list of the people who come, other leaders and even other groups. Put the list where you will see it daily (in your Bible?) and pray for them.
- Use the word of God to pray – this helps avoid mental drift and ensures biblical praying. It allows God to set the agenda for your prayers. Pray for people along the lines of the main point of each session. Philippians 1:9-11 is a great prayer to pray for the whole group.
- Pray specifically and expectantly. God loves to answer prayers, and, if you pray for specific things to happen, and for particular problems to be resolved, you will be encouraged as you see God answering.

GETTING TO KNOW YOUR FELLOW LEADERS

You will be praying, studying and teaching your group together, so it's important to get to know each other before you begin. Meet together and work out who will be taking particular responsibility for looking after people who are in the group. The quality of your love, respect and fellowship with others in the leadership team is an important part of how the group will see what it means to be a disciple.

PREPARE FOR PASTORAL PROBLEMS

People often come to Christ in very messy circumstances. These will not resolve automatically or immediately. Some will take a considerable amount of thought, time, prayer and encouragement before they are resolved. Try to anticipate the pastoral issues that are likely to arise for the people in your group and how you will deal with them. Think about how you would help people with these issues and which parts of the Bible will be particularly relevant to them.

Meet with your co-leaders to discuss how you might handle some of the issues listed on the next page. It is important to know when it is right to pass on these difficulties to someone who is more experienced at dealing with them, or to involve a health professional or a suitable trained counsellor.

How would you help a person who was...

- *sleeping with a partner?*
- *dealing with addictions?*
- *unsure that God can forgive them for something they've done?*
- *coping with broken family relationships?*
- *dating a non-Christian girlfriend or boyfriend?*
- *worried that they are not a Christian?*
- *rejected by non-Christian friends or family?*
- *struggling with bad debt or unemployment?*
- *wrestling with same-sex attraction?*

BEFORE THE COURSE

Introducing Philippians

WHO WROTE PHILIPPIANS?

The apostle Paul wrote the letter to the Philippians. Not only is Paul's writing style much in evidence, but the early church unanimously declared it to be his work.

WHERE WAS IT WRITTEN?

Philippians 1:13-14 tells us that Paul wrote the letter while in prison, most likely when he was under house arrest in Rome.

Acts 28:14-31 reveals some fascinating details about this period of Paul's life: he was allowed to live by himself in his own rented house, albeit with a soldier to guard him. He was also free to receive visitors, preaching and teaching "boldly and without hindrance" (Acts 28:31).

WHEN WAS IT WRITTEN?

The evidence suggests that it was written around AD 61.

WHO WAS PAUL WRITING TO?

All the Christians in Philippi and their leaders. The city of Philippi in Greece was a successful Roman colony, whose inhabitants prided themselves on being Roman citizens. Many Philippians made a point of speaking Latin, and even dressed like Romans.

Read the background to the church in Philippi in Acts 16. Reflect on Paul's relationship with the church in Philippi – the following questions may help:

- ***Describe the circumstances around the birth of the church in Philippi.***
- ***Who was in the church and what was their background (social, religious etc)?***
- ***Who were the leaders of the church?***
- ***How long did Paul spend in Philippi?***
- ***What was the situation when Paul left? Or why did he leave?***
- ***What pressures might the church have faced after Paul left?***

WHY WAS PHILIPPIANS WRITTEN?

Paul wanted to thank the Philippian Christians for their "partnership in the gospel" (1:5), including the gift they had sent him when they found out he had been put in prison. But Paul does several other things too:

- he reports on his present circumstances;
- he encourages them to stand firm and to rejoice in the face of persecution;
- he urges them to be humble and united;
- he warns them against certain dangerous people within their church (see Philippians 3);
- and he sends Epaphroditus back home to Philippi.

WHAT IS DISTINCTIVE ABOUT THE LETTER?

Philippians is a radical picture of what it means to be a Christian: self-humbling (2:1-4), single-minded (3:13-14), anxiety-free (4:6), and able to do all things (4:13).

Unusually, Philippians contains no Old Testament quotations. This may have been because there was no Jewish synagogue in Philippi.

It is also the New Testament letter of joy: the word, in its various forms, occurs 16 times in Philippians.

Read the whole letter through twice and answer the following questions:

- ***What are the main themes?***
- ***What is the overall structure of the letter?***
- ***What do we learn about the church in Philippi?***
- ***What context is the letter written into?***
- ***What difficulties is the church facing?***
- ***What are the strengths and weaknesses of the church?***

In order to familiarize yourself further with Philippians, you will find it helpful to read a commentary. We recommend the following:

- Gordon Fee: **IVP New Testament Commentary – Philippians**
  Free online at www.biblegateway.com/resources/commentaries/
- Ralph Martin: **Tyndale New Testament Commentary – Philippians**
- Don Carson: **Basics for Believers**
  This is a book you could recommend to group members if their English is good enough.

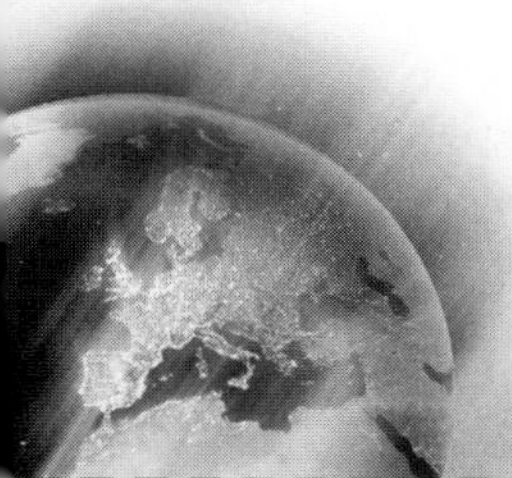

BEFORE THE COURSE

Running the sessions

PREPARING BEFORE THE GROUP ARRIVES

Arrive in plenty of time so that you can pray with the other leaders. Pray for individual participants, asking God to help them grasp the truths that will be presented that week. Pray too for one another.

It may be helpful each week to use one of Paul's prayers as a model for your own. Try praying through:

Week 1: 1 Thessalonians 5:23-24
Week 2: Ephesians 1:17-19
Week 3: 2 Thessalonians 1:11-12
Week 4: Philemon 4-6
Week 5: 2 Thessalonians 2:16-17
Week 6: Ephesians 3:16-19
Week 7: 1 Thessalonians 3:12-13
Week 8: Colossians 1:9-12

PREPARING THE ROOM

Think about the type of people coming and make them feel as relaxed as possible. Make sure they know where the toilet is. Think about...

- **Seating.** Are there any special seating needs for the guests (bad backs, older people who don't want to be seated too low)? People with hearing problems might need to be nearer the leader. If you are using the DVD, everyone needs to see the screen comfortably. Some groups might enjoy a more 'seminar-style' format where people sit around a table to discuss. This makes it easier to juggle Bibles and Study Guides.

- **Lighting**. Check that it is adequate so people can see the booklet.

- **Room temperature**. Make sure it is comfortable before people arrive.

- **Pets**. Put them in another room until you know if all the guests are comfortable with them.

You could put on some fairly neutral background music – popular jazz is often a good option. Be careful of pushing your particular eccentric tastes in music. But remember, this is to be in the background to set the atmosphere – not too loud or it will make chatting together difficult. Turn the music off when you get started.

If you are preparing a meal, check if people have any dietary requirements. Avoid pork and beef with people from a Muslim, Jewish or Hindu background. If you are not sharing a meal together, have a pot of coffee/tea ready, a jug of fruit juice and some water.

Think of some subjects to talk about beforehand so that, as you are drinking and waiting for others to arrive, there won't be embarrassing silences. You may not need them, but be prepared.

WELCOMING PARTICIPANTS

- **Remember their names.** This makes people feel valued and respected. Use name badges if it makes this easier.
- **Take the lead in introducing people to each other.** Always introduce new participants. If you know some background that is relevant, then use that too. 'Let me introduce you to Fred. He works in the building trade too.' 'Li is from S Korea and is studying Mathematics.' 'Sarah has two boys at Bean Road School as well.'
- Make sure there is time for people to relax and talk to each other before you begin. This greatly helps the discussion later.

If you are eating together, the meal is a great opportunity to model the importance of giving thanks to God. One of the leaders should be ready to give thanks each week for the food that has been prepared.

Sit where you can see everyone. That way, you can make eye contact with people, and it also ensures that they can see you too. It's not a good idea for leaders to sit next to one another, as this can look intimidating. Why not save your seat before others arrive, with your Bible or jacket.

LEADING THE BIBLE STUDY

After everyone has arrived and you've had time to relax and chat together over a meal, begin the Bible study time. As leader, your responsibility is more than just asking the Bible study questions. You should try to maintain a relaxed atmosphere and involve everyone in the discussion if possible. Don't forget how important the tone of your voice and your body language can be as you lead the discussion.

Each study follows the same pattern:

- **Discuss any questions.** At the start of the study ask participants if they have any questions or issues that have arisen from their **The Week Ahead** readings and discuss as necessary.
- **Recap.** Briefly summarise last week's study.
- **Opening discussion question(s).** These questions are designed to open up discussion. Don't spend too long over them. The aim is just to get people talking.
- **Read aloud from Philippians.** It is a good idea to involve the participants by dividing the passage between them and asking them to read a few verses each aloud. Be very aware of anyone who might not be comfortable doing this –

especially in the first couple of weeks. Once they have read the passage aloud, let them read it again silently. If anyone has English as a second language, encourage them to read the passage in their own language too.

- **Bible words.** These word lists pick out difficult words from the passage in Philippians and define them in simple English. It is a good idea to make sure that everyone understands these words before starting the Bible Study questions. You will know your group. If they need you to go through the words one at a time, do it, but if not, keep going. If you have some members who are not struggling with English and some who are, ask the confident ones to help those who are struggling.
- **Questions on Philippians.** The passage is usually split into smaller sections to make the study easier. It is worth reading each section again. This helps in terms of language, and encourages students to look to Scripture for the answers.

  It is important to listen carefully to the answers given and to reply graciously. Your group need to know that they are valued and that their opinions are important to you. Encourage them to write down the answers in the space provided in their Study Guide. Notes on the answers are provided for you in the second section of this Leader's Guide, but it's a good idea to write your own notes into a Study Guide, so that you can work from the same book as your group.
- **Pray.** At the end of the study give members a chance to write down things they would like to pray for. Space is provided for this on the last page of each study. For ideas on how to encourage internationals to pray, see page 32.

PRAYER TIME

Philippians will provoke and challenge even the most mature Christians so it will be appropriate to pray at the end of the study. There are a number of different ways you might approach this, depending on how confident your group are.

- You might, in the first couple of weeks, choose simply to pray on behalf of the whole group about the issues that have been raised in Philippians. Keep your prayers simple and model to your group how to pray.
- Alternatively, you might ask each group member in turn what they would like prayer for, and then pray on behalf of the whole group. As the weeks move on you could split the group up and ask them to pray for one another. This may help them feel confident to pray out loud.
- For groups who are able, encourage praying aloud for one another. Ask them to pray in their own language and to use the section provided in their Study Guide to write down their prayers. It is important that by the end of the course all participants should be willing to pray in this way.

FINISHING

- **DVD.** At the end of the prayer time, you could show the DVD as a summary of what you have been discussing.

- **Always finish at the promised time.** Good timekeeping develops trust in the group, and people will be more likely to return next week. However, let participants know that they are welcome to stay and talk further if they like. As the course progresses, many participants will need your advice and support as they seek to serve Christ wholeheartedly.
- **Limit the study time to one and a half to two hours.** You should be able to complete the study and pray in that time, but if you are behind schedule, don't rush through the questions. Instead, complete as many as you can and consider finishing the study at the start of your next meeting.

THE WEEK AHEAD

Download and print out **The Week Ahead** studies for each member of your group (available for free download from www.discipleshipexplored.org). Encourage participants to use these studies as their daily readings for the coming week. These studies are designed to help participants establish a pattern of daily Bible reading and prayer. Explain that you'll also be doing the studies yourself and that there will be time to discuss them briefly next week. You may want to introduce quickly what the studies will be about as a way of encouraging your group to do them.

Go through **The Week Ahead** studies as your own daily readings. If you fill in the answers yourself, you will be more able to help the participants understand the passages they have been reading. Again, if you show enthusiasm and a willingness to spend time doing this, they will follow your lead. Be excited about what you have learned and mention it as part of your prayer requests.

DECIDE HOW YOU WILL USE THE EXTRAS

There are two extra sessions available for use in this course.

- **Introduction to Philippians:** The first is an introductory session, developed by Kerry Fee, a staff worker with Friends International. This session is designed to introduce people to the basic ideas of how to understand a Bible passage, and particularly a New Testament letter. If your group has people who might appreciate and cope with this level of teaching, then use this as an introductory session before the main *Discipleship Explored* sessions start. The leader's notes, worksheets and a powerpoint presentation for the session can be downloaded from www.discipleshipexplored.org
- **An example to follow:** There is one part of Philippians – 2:19-30 – that is deliberately not covered in the 8 main sessions (in order to finish the course in eight weeks). At the end of the Study Guide, we have included a shorter section with questions on this passage. You can choose to use this in one of three ways:
  1. Suggest that people do it at home one week;
  2. Do the study together at its natural point between weeks 4 and 5;
  3. Use it as an "Extra" at the end of the eight main sessions.

  Because this study is shorter, it provides the opportunity to use it in a different way e.g. over a more elaborate meal, as part of a celebration "party", or with an extra time for questions, testimonies etc.

What to do if...

... THERE'S SILENCE

If a question is met with silence, don't be too quick to speak. Allow people time to think. They might be considering how to phrase their answer. Remember that in some cultures it is considered rude to speak immediately after the previous person; therefore a short silence (even up to 30 seconds) is the polite norm.

If you sense that someone knows the answer but is shy about giving it, ask them by name. Often they will be happy to be asked.

It might be appropriate to try a "game" – asking them to raise their hand if they agree or disagree with certain answers as you give them.

It may help to divide people into groups of two or three to work through questions and then have them feed their answers back to the whole group.

... ONE PERSON ANSWERS ALL THE QUESTIONS

- Thank them for their answers. Try asking the group: "What do other people think?"
- Direct a few questions at the other participants by name. (But if it seems awkward, open up the question to the rest of the group.)
- Sit beside the talkative participant the following week. That will make it harder for them to catch your eye and answer the questions.
- If the situation continues, you may need to say something to the participant after the study and ask them to give others an opportunity to answer next time. For example: "Thank you so much for everything you are contributing. I wonder if you could help me with the quieter people in the group..."

... SOMEONE GIVES THE WRONG ANSWER

- **Do not immediately correct them.** Give the person the opportunity to correct themselves. Ask them, for example: "What does verse 4 tell us about that?" If they are still unable to answer correctly, give others the chance (for example: "Does anyone disagree or want to add anything?").
- **Graciously correct.** If necessary, don't be afraid graciously to correct a wrong

answer that may mislead others. Say something like: "Thank you, that's an interesting point, but I'm not sure that's what's going on here."

- **Have further questions in mind** to develop the initial answer. For example: "What did you mean by that?" or "What does everyone else think?" or "Where does it say that?" If no one is able to answer the question, give the correct answer, showing from the Bible passage why it is the right answer.

... SOMEONE ASKS A QUESTION YOU CANNOT ANSWER

- **Lead honestly.** You won't be able to answer every question. Some questions can be easily addressed, but others will be difficult. If you don't know the answer, say so – but tell them that you'll try to have an answer ready for the following week.
- **Lend a book.** It may be best to give them a suitable book to help them. See www.discipleshipexplored.org/reading for suggestions.

... PARTICIPANTS DON'T COME BACK

If you've already established a good relationship with that person, contact him or her once to say you missed them and that it would be great to see them next week, but don't put pressure on them.

... PARTICIPANTS MISS A WEEK OR MORE

Welcome them back and during the meal try and summarise what they have missed. Encourage them to read the passages in Philippians they have missed and to work through the questions in the Study Guide as their daily reading. Let them know that they can come back to you with anything they are concerned about or do not understand.

... IT BECOMES APPARENT THAT THE PARTICIPANT IS NOT A CHRISTIAN

If they have not already attended *Christianity Explored*, explain that it may be more useful as an introduction for them and take them to the next available course meeting. If the next course does not start for some time, consider meeting with them on an individual basis and taking them through *Christianity Explored.*

If they have already been through *Christianity Explored*, then don't worry. As long as they aren't keeping the group from learning, let them carry on attending. They are hearing God's word, and that will do its work (Isaiah 55:10-11). Moreover, the Christians in the group will be learning to model the Christian life and that will impact them as well. Where appropriate, take the opportunity to explain the gospel and if possible try and get the Christians in the group to explain it to the others.

If they are preventing the group from learning, it may be appropriate to pull them out of the group and meet on a one-to-one basis to study a Gospel together.

... THE PARTICIPANTS DON'T APPEAR TO BE GROWING

Remember that no matter how much Bible knowledge we have, or how faultless our lives are, only God can enable our participants to mature as Christians. We need to allow God to work in his time and in his way ("I planted the seed, Apollos watered it, but God made it grow" 1 Corinthians 3:6).

If the Bible is being read and explained, and we are praying that they will grow, then we can leave it to God to do the rest.

... THE PASTORAL ISSUE THEY CONFIDE IN YOU IS NOT ONE YOU ARE QUALIFIED TO DEAL WITH

It is best not to try and deal with situations if you feel you are out of your depth. Encourage the person to go with you to see your pastor or a Christian counsellor.

Pray with them about the issue.

Do not break their confidence without asking their permission first. However, in extreme circumstances you may need to do so even if they refuse to give you permission.

LEADERSHIP SKILLS

Working with English speakers

The *Discipleship Explored* Universal Edition has been developed for use with a wide range of people. The questions and explanations have been written to be simple, but not shallow. We have not "dumbed down" the content, even if we have tried to express it in clear language. So we hope that this resource will find wide use with people who are native English speakers. But we hope that it will also prove useful to those with limited literary skills, who might not be used to reading much.

A few things to bear in mind are:

ATMOSPHERE

Some people are easily intimidated by the idea of studying, for practical and/or cultural reasons, so it will be important to avoid a classroom atmosphere.

- Think about how you arrange your venue – comfortable and informal rather than functional and formal.
- Be warm and friendly, and use humour. Reassure people that there are no exams or marks, and no passing or failing involved in *Discipleship Explored*.
- Be clear in your own mind about the goal of *Discipleship Explored* but flexible about how that goal is achieved (e.g. not everyone needs to write down answers in their booklets).
- Try to avoid using educational terms with reference to *Discipleship Explored* (see table below).

Avoid...	Use...
study	look at
a study, a Bible study	a session
course	*Discipleship Explored*
students	group members, guests, people
teacher	group leader
homework	preparing for next session

Note: *If your group is made up of internationals who are learning English, they will be very comfortable with the idea of a course of study etc. and may be attracted to joining your group for this reason.*

OPPORTUNITIES TO PREPARE

It's possible that people in your group may be unwilling to answer any questions in the session, however much you try to rephrase things or give them ideas. This may simply be due to a lack of confidence, rather than lack of understanding. What can sometimes be helpful is the opportunity to go through the questions and, if people wish, to write down some answers in their booklet before coming to the session.

They will need to get hold of the booklet in time to prepare for the first session. You could hold an introductory session to introduce yourself and any helpers, the venue, *Discipleship Explored*, and the members of the group to each other. (If your group has people who might appreciate and cope with this level of teaching, see page 22 for information about an optional opening session, "Introduction to Philippians".) This would be an ideal opportunity for people to be given the Study Guide to prepare the first session.

Make this optional for those who will find it beneficial. Some will not bother, some will take the opportunity just to read through the Bible passage and questions, while some will try to complete the whole session. Make sure they understand that no one is going to "mark" their answers. To answer the questions in the booklet, people will need to read the Bible passage, so make sure they know where to find it.

READING AND WRITING

If your group have limited literacy skills, any reading aloud should be done by the group leader or someone who helps you with the group and is good at reading aloud. Never expect the people in your group do this. It would be good to read aloud both the Bible passage and the questions in the booklet.

Some people may be intimidated by having to handle a whole Bible packed with small type. We have prepared sheets of the individual NIV passages in Philippians in a reader-friendly format that you can download and print out. Visit www.discipleshipexplored.org. Encourage your group to underline, circle or highlight key words and phrases, so that they can more easily read and understand the passage. If the group struggles with NIV, we suggest you try either NIrV or NCV.

Any writing should also be optional. People may have a lot of difficulty with writing and may prefer to do any out of sight of the group. Provide pens and pencils in a central, easily accessible place, rather than allocating one to each person, so that people don't feel they are expected to write something.

BREAKS

Providing breaks will be more important for some groups than others. Be aware that some people may find the session quite intensive and tiring, especially if they have no experience of church or of meeting with Christians. Allow a few moments for people to go outside to smoke a cigarette, use the toilets or just stretch their legs and get some fresh air.

Cross-cultural discipleship

If you are involved with cross-cultural discipleship, there will be some practical issues that you need to think about before you begin the course.

Crucially, you will need to keep in mind at all times that those in your group live between two cultures, two sets of values, two ways of living. You will therefore have to address the topics raised during this course in both contexts.

This is important because, without appropriate discipleship, people will struggle to maintain their faith and share it with others when they return home. Experience has shown that if they are not expecting and not equipped to deal with their return home, then a large proportion will not be living the Christian life at all, and moreover may not even be claiming to be Christians any more. Obviously, things will differ for each individual case but there are some basic principles that you can apply.

Remember that our culture affects our identity from the core of our being to our external actions. Our understanding of who we are is deeply affected by the culture in which we grew up. Much of Western society is founded on the core idea/value of individualism, i.e. from childhood people are taught the principle "I am because I am". The most important thing is to "be yourself". Being independent is seen as a commendable quality. Much of the Western education system is aimed at teaching children to become independent. They are taught that their opinion matters, therefore in a discussion group everyone's contribution is valuable and should be expressed. This is why, for example, most westerners do not have a problem disagreeing with their teacher.

In many cultures around the world, people's core understanding of who they are is based on a different premise: "I am because we are" is the core value/idea. Therefore, the primary commitment in people's morals is to the group that they belong to (family, ethnic group etc). To look after your group is the most important thing to do.

When people become Christians, it is not simply their external actions that need to be transformed, it is their whole understanding of their identity. If the gospel only affects the externals, then we have a problem. Christianity is not an extra layer to be added to our identity – but needs to be at the core of our identity.

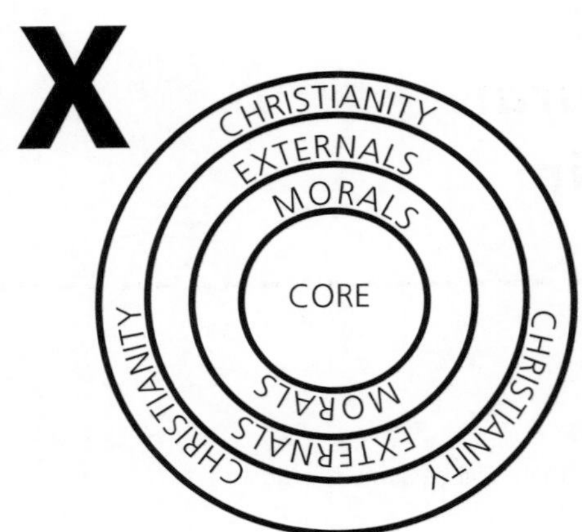

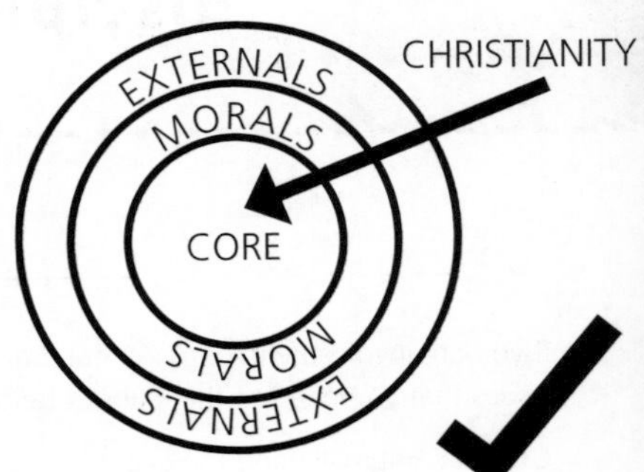

If people live for any period of time outside their own culture, they begin to take on some of the externals of their host culture or even adopt some of the morals. For example, an international student in the UK may become more individualistic. They might learn to challenge their lecturers when they think they are wrong. But when they return home, they quickly discover that the way they think and act causes friction with people back home. So, in time, people usually decide to adapt back to the cultural norm.

Now, if our international student becomes a Christian while studying in the UK, we have to ask ourselves: will they see their faith as something that is bound to their British culture, something that can be discarded when the going gets tough? Or has their discipleship helped them to grapple with how the gospel affects every area of their life right to their core understanding of who they are? Is their new identity in Christ or is it in their culture? If their faith has not penetrated to the core, then, when the going gets tough, it will be discarded along with the elements of British culture that have caused them so much trouble as they adapt to life back home.

If we disciple people effectively, then Christianity will not be an added-on external layer but an integral part of their identity. Their identity has to be in Christ if they are to persevere in the midst of the difficult transition back to their home country. This means that we must attempt to narrow the perceived gap between their understanding of what it means to be a Christian in the two cultures they live between.

You will most likely be leading a group from many different cultures. This will mean that each individual, as well as yourself, will bring their own cultural values and views into play when answering the questions or even deciding on how to behave within the group. It is impractical, and in many cases impossible, to learn

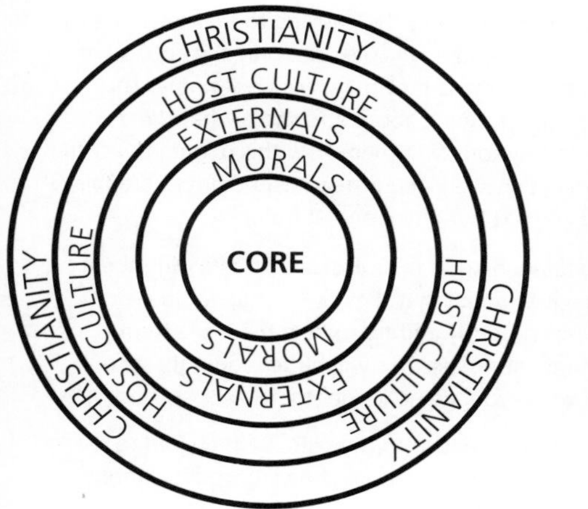

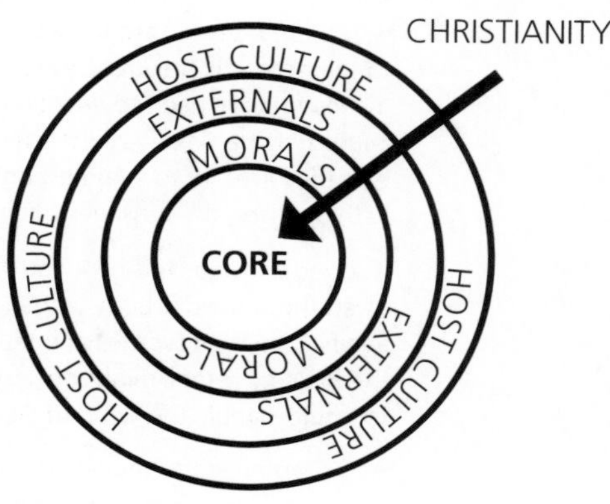

all you can about each culture and hope that means you can lead the group more effectively. It is far better to work from a series of basic principles that will apply to leading any group.

As you work through Philippians, you want the group to understand what it means to live for Christ and to find their identity secure in him. As you do this, here are some things to think about:

HELP THEM READ THE BIBLE FOR THEMSELVES

Modelling good Bible-reading practice is the primary way they will learn how to faithfully handle the word of God.

First, having worked through the book of Philippians, you should then easily be able to encourage them to systematically read through other books of the Bible. Secondly, the **Week Ahead studies** will show them how to set a topic in the context of the rest of the Bible.

The way you handle the Bible will affect them – so think carefully and prayerfully about how you approach the Bible. Not only will this affect them but, when they return home, they will pass on your practices, and even your bad habits, to others.

There is a list of helpful books on this topic on the recommended reading list at www.discipleshipexplored.org

TEACH THEM TO APPLY THE BIBLE TO THEIR LIVES

As we approach the Bible studies that make up *Discipleship Explored,* it is vital to remember that our primary task is to clearly and faithfully explain the passage, in order to make sure that those in our group understand what the passage says in context. The Bible study questions and notes you have will help you do this.

There are also questions that help the group apply the passage to their own lives. It is in these questions that we need to make sure we cover not only the application to their present circumstances but also to those they may face back home. This means that we need to encourage them to think about and share what those issues may be. Take time to listen and explore with them how this might impact the way they live. Try to avoid giving direct answers and instead help them to grapple with applying the passage to their context both here and at home.

It sounds obvious but be aware that laughing at their answers or criticizing them (even through your body language) may mean that they will not open up ever again. Take their worries and feelings seriously and try to help them see from the Bible how they might deal with those issues. This will better equip them to faithfully handle the word of God when you are no longer there.

Again, you need to model applying the Bible to your own life. Be prepared to share your own answers and struggles with the group, always showing from Scripture why you think and behave as you do.

Try to encourage the group to be accountable to one another as they learn to live for Christ. You will need to develop the sort of atmosphere where this is possible.

GET THEM TO STUDY THE BIBLE AND PRAY IN THEIR OWN LANGUAGE

If we are using English as the only language when we study the Bible, worship and pray, then our group will struggle when they get back home. If they cannot communicate the gospel and concepts they have learned in their own language, then they will struggle to fit in and others will see their beliefs as a "Western message". Ensure they have a copy of the Bible in their own language and encourage them to use it during the group study as well as in their **Week Ahead** daily Bible reading. Bilingual Bibles are available in some languages – see www.discipleshipexplored.org for help on where to get these. There are also online versions that can be printed out – again see the website for details.

You will find it much easier to lead the Bible studies if your participants have read the passages in their own language. You may find that some people are unwilling to do this because they want to improve their English – however it is vital to help them see that they will be better able to serve Christ if they can talk about him in both languages.

It is also extremely helpful not only to encourage them to pray in their own language and style during the prayer time at the end of the studies, but if they can to pray with another Christian in their own language. It will again help them to fit in better back home. You may find an unwillingness to do this because of the desire to learn English. In this case, try and encourage them to pray in their own language and then translate for the group.

ENCOURAGE GROUP DISCUSSION

You may find that some people in the group are unwilling to speak up and enter the group discussions. This could be because of their cultural background and expectations of how they should participate within a group. You may find it useful to set out some parameters and let them know what is expected of the group. Explain that the study is a discussion, not a lecture, and tell them it is important for them to share their ideas and questions. Tell them that you are not expecting them to always have the correct answer and that no question is too simple or difficult. They will find it easier to participate if this is made clear.

If you find the group dynamic still does not work, it may be that people are only used to group discussion in a single-sex environment. You may want to consider splitting them into single-sex groups.

ENCOURAGE THEM TO SERVE

Those who practice their gifts while here, use them back home. Don't fall into the trap of treating them as guests who have nothing to give. Help them to identify an area of service where they can use their talents, personalities and gifts to serve the wider church. The best place to start is within the group itself. For example, get them involved in making refreshments, in setting up the room, organizing social events and so on. You are in an ideal position to help them find opportunities to serve in their local church or Christian Union or fellowship (for example: playing an instrument, leading a small group, organizing or participating in outreach events and so on).

HELP THEM TO SHARE THE GOSPEL

The need to share the gospel with others will emerge strongly as you work through Philippians. Again, if they do not start to evangelize here, then they will be unlikely to do it at home. You need to make it clear that the gospel is for everyone and that the Bible commands all Christians to evangelize. It is exciting to think that those in your group will be able to share their faith in countries where you may be unable even to visit.

BE AWARE OF SPIRITUAL WARFARE

The Bible is clear that there is a spiritual battle being fought (Ephesians 6:10-13). Don't be naive about, or frightened by, the power the devil is able to manifest. Those in your group may well have first-hand experience of this or know someone who has. Be sensitive to their feelings and fears. Some of their apprehensions may be misguided but others may be very real. It takes tremendous courage for them to say anything about this in the first place, so don't dismiss it.

Encourage them to see what Scripture has to say about this (e.g. Revelation 12:11; Ephesians 1:20-21; 1 John 4:4) and most especially help them to understand that because of Christ they don't need to fear the devil. Explain that they must deal with this now. The best thing you can do is point people to Scripture, praying with them and for them.

HELP THEM TO THINK ABOUT THEIR RETURN HOME

Studying the Bible is the best possible preparation for returning home. There are, however, a lot of other issues they will need to think about. The website www.discipleshipexplored.org suggests some helpful reading matter. It is good to start this process one to two months before they return home, which may mean you need to do it while they are on *Discipleship Explored*.

Think Home is a booklet designed to help prepare internationals students in the UK for their return home. Further details from the Friends International website (www.friendsinternational.org.uk).

You never stop learning to be a disciple

You need to be planning what follows from an early stage so that people are not left with nothing to slot into when the time comes. It may be that there will be different things that are appropriate for different members.

- For some who have become Christians and have matured in their faith, it may be possible for them to join the regular home Bible-study programme of the church.
- For those who have yet to become Christians, there many be a further course or study group organised which will retain an evangelistic and exploratory style, as they continue to think through the gospel and their response to it.
- For international students who have a limited time in your country, you should think through what might be the best preparation for them before they return. Perhaps a Bible-overview course, or a study of the Acts of the Apostles.
- If your group has "bonded", there is a good argument for continuing to meet together and perhaps growing the group into a more regular Bible-study and fellowship group. However, although they will be comfortable with one another, they will miss interaction with the wider church family.

It is particularly important to support your participants if they are internationals who will be returning home (see "Cross-cultural Discipleship" on page 29 of this book). You will need to help them find a church and remain in contact with them as they go back to a family and a cultural environment that may be hostile to their new faith. Go to the *Discipleship Explored* website (www.discipleshipexplored.org) for some information on how to find a church that will continue to teach and nurture them when they go home.

Other things to note about continued support for your group:

- **Reading.** There are plenty of books that are suitable for new believers, including:
  Understanding the Bible by John Stott, which gives an overview of the Bible. It is available in many other languages.
  The Stranger on the Road to Emmaus by John R Cross is an illustrated book that takes you through the Bible story. It is also available in many other languages.
  Dig Deeper by Nigel Beynon and Andrew Sach is a helpful book giving a number of 'tools' you can use to understand a Bible passage.
  Think Home is a booklet designed to help prepare international students in the UK for their return home. Available from www.friendsinternational.org.uk

- **Regular personal Bible-study notes.** These are widely available, many of them in multiple languages. Visit www.discipleshipexplored.org for recommendations.
- **Service.** Part of being a disciple of Jesus Christ is to give time and effort to encouraging and supporting God's people. Try to think about opportunities to get your group serving now, rather than being passive receivers – even if it is something very simple, like volunteering to help with coffee or gardening at church. Getting young disciples into the habit of being part of the crew, rather than just passengers, is really important.
- **Evangelism.** New Christians are often in a much better situation to be natural evangelists than those who have been Christians for a long time. They will have larger networks of non-Christian friends, and the change in their thinking and behaviour as they grow as believers will provoke comment and questions. Even if they struggle to tell others the gospel because they are timid or lack the understanding, encourage the group to be "invitational evangelists" by bringing their friends and family along to the next *Christianity Explored* group.
- **Writing.** Take note of Paul's example. He wrote many letters to teach and encourage the new Christians he knew – Philippians is one of them! Keep in touch with your group members, and become a lifelong friend, mentor and support to them.

SECTION 2

Study Guide

AS YOU START THE COURSE

Before we begin

As you start *Discipleship Explored* you will need to introduce Paul's letter to your group. This letter was written 2000 years ago by Paul to a group of new Christians in Philippi.

- Use the map on page 4 of the Study Guide to show your group where Philippi is – a city in Greece.
- Read through the introduction on page 4 with them, and try to help them see that this is a letter from a real person to real people, even though it was a long time ago.
- Encourage your group that what this letter contains is important for them, because Paul is explaining how to live as a disciple of Jesus in every age and culture – not just his own.
- If you have time, read through Acts chapter 16, which has some wonderful stories of the first Christians in Philippi. Notice how the gospel was received by a wide variety of people:
    - Lydia – a wealthy international businesswoman
    - An un-named slave girl – from the lowest level of society
    - A jailer and his family – probably an ex-soldier and therefore a tough and self-reliant man.
- Try to convey some of the excitement of what this letter contains for your group. Over the next few weeks you will be discovering life-changing truths that will be the basic building blocks for understanding what it means to be a disciple of Jesus Christ.

Note: In the notes that follow, the text shown in the light grey boxes is the material that appears in the Study Guide used by group members.

WEEK 1: PHILIPPIANS 1:1-11

How can I be sure I'm a Christian?

To start the session, ask the group one of the following questions:

For a brand new group

- ***Why have you joined this Discipleship Explored group?***

For an existing group

- ***We are going to study Philippians together. What are you hoping to learn?***

For a group that may contain Christians and non-Christians

- ***Some of you may have questions about the Christian faith that you are hoping will be answered by being part of this group. If you have one, can you tell us about it?***

Make a note of these questions so that you can address them in future weeks. Don't try to answer them immediately. Your aim in the first session is to learn more about the group members, encourage them to take part in the discussion, and to help them enjoy being part of the group, so that they will want to return next week.

Leader's checklist

Have you...

- ☐ Made it clear to people the time and place where you will meet?
- ☐ Prepared food and drinks?
- ☐ Sufficient Bibles or printed out sheets with the Bible passages on them?
- ☐ The optional Discipleship Explored DVD ready to play?
- ☐ Printed out the daily study material (if you are going to use it)?
- ☐ Thought through your answers to each of the questions?
- ☐ Prayed for each group member and yourself as the leader?

OPENING DISCUSSION QUESTION

What would you write to your friends if you were unfairly put in prison?

Have an answer of your own ready, so that you can start the discussion if no one else is willing to talk.

Read aloud Philippians 1:1-11

If your group members have English as a second language, encourage *them to read the passage a second time in their own language. This will help them to better understand the passage but it will also help them if and when they return home—**see page 32.*

There is a list of Bible words from this week's passage (NIV) on pages 6-7 of the Bible study booklet. Depending on your group, it may be appropriate to go through some or all of these words at this point. The word list for this study is also shown below.

Bible words

v1 Christ. This name means "the chosen king". The same word in Hebrew is "Messiah". There are many promises in the Old Testament about the Christ/Messiah. They show that he would be God's chosen king.

v1 saints. Holy ones; those who God has set apart for himself. Every Christian is a saint.

v1 overseers and deacons. Church leaders.

v2 grace. God's gift of forgiveness to people who do not deserve it.

v2 peace. Peace with God.

v2 Lord. Master.

v5 gospel. The good news about Jesus Christ.

v6 day of Christ. The day when Jesus Christ will return to judge the world. (See verse 10 also.)

v7 confirming. Showing something is true.

v8 testify. Be a witness. A witness tells others the truth about something that they have seen or heard.

v8 I long for all of you.
I want to be with you.

v8 with the affection of Christ Jesus.
With the love of Jesus.

v9 abound. Increase.

v9 insight. Being able to understand something clearly.

v10 discern. Understand or judge correctly.

v10 pure and blameless. Someone who does not think wrong things or do wrong things.

v11 fruit. Results.

v11 righteousness. Goodness that is good enough for God. You must be perfect and have no sin to be good enough for God. Jesus Christ is the only person who has ever been perfect.

Re-read Philippians 1:1-2

Verse 1 is like the envelope of the letter. It shows who it is from and who it is going to.

Optional: You could show a letter to the group, and point out the address on the front and the return address.

1 ***Who is the letter from and who was it sent to?***

The letter is from Paul and Timothy. It was sent to the saints (TNIV: God's holy people), overseers and deacons in Philippi.

Follow-up questions

- ***Who was Paul?***

Acts 9. Paul was a Jewish teacher who tried to stop Christians from teaching about Jesus. But then he became a Christian himself, and travelled around spreading the message about Jesus. On one of his journeys, he went to Philippi and started the church there (Acts 16). Later on, he was put in prison for teaching about Jesus.

- ***Who was Timothy?***

Acts 16:1-3. Timothy was a young Christian man who travelled with Paul when he went to Philippi. He was known to the Philippians. Later on, he became the leader of the church in Ephesus.

- ***What do we know about Philippi?***

Philippi was a Roman colony, and a prosperous trading city in ancient Greece. *See the map on page 4 of the Bible study booklet.*

2 *What does Paul say about himself and Timothy?*

They are servants of Christ Jesus. In verse 1, the word "servant" literally means "slave". Paul sees himself as a slave of Jesus.

Optional follow-up question

- ***Does this surprise you?***

3 *What does Paul call the readers of the letter?*

"Saints in Christ Jesus at Philippi."

- ***What does the word "saint" mean?***

If necessary, refer the group to the word list on page 6 of the Study Guide.

The popular view of a saint is either someone who is especially good, patient and unselfish, or a historical person who is worshipped or greatly respected. However, the Bible uses the word "saint" to describe believers in Jesus. Every Christian is a saint. So Paul is writing to all the Christians in Philippi.

Read Philippians 1:3-8

Note: Reading the passage again will help the group members to focus their answers on the passage.

(4) *How does Paul feel about the Philippian Christians? Why?*

He is thankful for them (verse 3). He is full of joy (verse 4).

Why? Because they were partners with him in sharing the gospel (verse 5). In other words, they were supporters of Paul as he told others the message about Jesus. What it means to be partners in the gospel will become clear in the rest of Philippians. He is confident that God will finish what he started in them (verse 6).

Paul is also encouraged by them, because he and the Philippians "share in God's grace" together (verse 7). This means he knows that they are all brothers and sisters in Christ. Paul feels so strongly about them because of the love of Jesus (verse 8).

"Partnership in the gospel" means that the Philippian Christians were working with Paul to tell other people about Jesus.

(5) *What is Paul confident about in verse 6?*

That God has started a work in them when they became Christians, and he will finish it. What God starts, he finishes.

Follow-up question

- ***What is the good work that God is going to complete in them?*** Salvation.

(6) *Is becoming a Christian an "inside change" or an "outside change"? Who makes the change? Why is it important to understand this?*

Becoming a Christian is an "inside change". It is God who makes the change (verse 6). It is God who makes us into followers of Jesus. This is important to understand. If it is just us who have made the decision to become Christians, we can easily choose to stop being a Christian. But what God starts, he finishes. If it is God who has begun to work in us, we can be confident that he will not let us slip away.

The "inside change" of becoming a Christian can be seen in an "outside change".

(7) *What "outside changes" showed Paul that God has begun his work in the Philippians (verse 5)?*

Their "partnership in the gospel" – which means that the Philippian Christians were working with Paul to tell other people about Jesus.
We will see other examples of "outside changes" later in the book of Philippians. For your information, these include:

- praying for Paul in prison (1:19)
- sending one of their members to help Paul (2:25)
- sending money and gifts to Paul (4:15-18)

8 ***Have you ever been unsure that you are a real Christian? What made you feel that way?***

Share your own experience (briefly). If you talk openly about times when you have had doubts, it makes it easier for the group to talk about their own doubts. The answer to these worries is verse 6. Our doubts have a common theme: they are about us – what we think, feel and do. Verse 6 tells us that the important thing is about God – what he has done. And God finishes what he starts.

? Optional follow-up question

- ***How can these verses help us if we are feeling unsure?***

Verse 6 – our confidence should be based on God's work in us, not on a choice we have made. What God starts, he finishes.

9 ***Have you seen any "outside changes" in your life since you became a Christian? What are they?***

Note: If you have non-Christians in your group, ask them: ***How do you think you might have to change if you became a Christian?***

There are lots of "inside changes" that God makes, but we can only tell they are real if they show on the outside.

- **We love the gospel message.** We show this by joining in telling others about Jesus and supporting those who preach the gospel ("partnership in the gospel", verse 5).
- **We love other Christians (verse 9).** We show this by wanting to meet with our brothers and sisters at church.
- **We have a new understanding of God (verse 9).** We show this by wanting to learn more – reading the Bible and joining study groups, like this one!

It is worth pointing out that people who are feeling doubtful often do not see what is clearer to others. If they feel and know they are sinful, it is a sign that God is at work in them. If they are at this study, it is a sign that they are hungry for the truth and want to spend time with other believers! You can encourage the group that they are already showing signs that God is at work in them because they are here!

Read Philippians 1:9-11

Paul knows that the Philippians, like all Christians, are not perfect. So he prays for them.

(10) ***What does Paul pray for and why?***

He prays that they would grow:
- in love.
- in understanding.
- in discernment.
- in righteousness.

A disciple of Jesus Christ is someone who is growing in these things.

Note: *The list above is taken from the NIV – other versions may phrase these verses differently. Check the version your group members will be using, so that you know what answers to expect.*

Follow-up question

- ***Why does Paul pray for these things?***

So that they would learn to live in a way that pleases God (verse 10). A disciple is a learner. A disciple does not just learn knowledge. A disciple is learning to live for Jesus Christ.

So that God will be glorified (verse 11).

(11) ***What does Paul hope will be the result of this (see verses 10-11)?***

He hopes that they will live in a way that is pleasing to God for the rest of their lives. And that people will praise God and give him glory as a result.

(12) ***Paul's prayer can help us to pray for other Christians and ourselves. What should we thank God for, and what should we ask him to do in our lives?***

Thank God for the work he has begun in us. Thank him that what he starts, he finishes. Ask God to help us grow in the ways listed in verses 9-11. If any members of the group are not yet Christians, ask God to help them to trust in Jesus.

MEMORY VERSE

"He who began a good work in you will carry it on to completion until the day of Christ Jesus." Philippians 1:6. At the end of each session we have included a memory verse taken from the Bible passage the group has studied. You may find it helpful to read this together as you finish the session. Ask your group members to learn this verse during the week – they may find it helpful to write it on a piece of card or in a notebook that they can carry around with them. If your group members have English as a second language, encourage them to learn the verse in their own language as well.

PRAY

Note: The members of your group might not be used to praying with others. The following suggestions may help:

- Ask them to pray aloud if they are able, since this helps and encourages the rest of the group. Reassure them that short, simple prayers are fine. It will help if you keep your own prayers short as well. Explain that the word "Amen" means "We agree". It is a way of everyone joining in with what has just been prayed.
- For suggestions on how to encourage internationals to pray, see page 32.
- Divide your group into pairs. Ask each member to use verses 9-11 to pray for their partner, personalizing the words with the other person's name.
- Give everyone a piece of paper (or use the "Things to pray for" box on page 8). Ask them to write down either a short prayer or an idea to turn into a prayer. Suggest a few things they might choose to pray about. Then ask each person to use what they have written to help them to pray aloud.

DVD

If you feel it's appropriate for your group, you may want to show the *Discipleship Explored* DVD at this point. The DVD can be used as a summary or as a refresher for the main teaching point in this session.

DAILY BIBLE STUDIES

We have prepared some simple daily Bible-reading notes for you to use with the group, which reinforce some of the truths that have been learned at this session, and encourage them to start a daily discipline of Bible reading and prayer. The notes are available for download from www.discipleshipexplored.org

Group members will benefit from the model of having a daily time with God. But use these notes with discretion – they may be too much for some to attempt.

CONCLUSION

Finish by encouraging your group members to come back next week. Tell them: "We've seen what starts to happen to someone who God has changed on the inside – next week we're going to see what a person looks like who God is turning into a real disciple..."

Additional notes for leaders

Why does Paul call Jesus "Christ Jesus", not "Jesus Christ"? These two phrases mean the same thing. "Christ" is not Jesus' surname, it is his title. "Christ" is a Greek word meaning "the anointed one". (The same word in the Hebrew language is "Messiah".) "Jesus" means "God saves". Paul uses the phrase "Christ Jesus" a lot in Philippians.

What does Paul mean by "partnership in the gospel"? At the moment, there is no need to unpack the idea of partnership in detail. It is enough to know that Paul is encouraged by their support. For your own interest, note that apart from the obvious support of prayer, and personal encouragement, this partnership was also very practical:

- **Acts 16** Lydia, the first convert in Philippi, opened her home to Paul and Timothy.
- **Philippians 2:25** They had sent one of their members – Epaphroditus – to look after Paul's needs.
- **Philippians 4:15-18** They were the only church that had sent Paul money and gifts to support him.

What is "the day of Christ Jesus"? "The day of Christ Jesus" (verse 6) and "the day of Christ" (verse 10) both mean the day when Christ will return to judge the world. The Bible makes it clear that this day will certainly come, but that we do not know when it will be (Matthew 24:36-44).

What can make you unsure that you are a real Christian? Doubts about whether we are real Christians come in many different ways:

- Sometimes this is about feelings. We still feel unforgiven, or sinful, or doubt that God could really love us. Some people expect to have amazing, instant experiences of God's love and warmth.
- Sometimes we have intellectual doubts: Does God exist? Am I just using Christianity as a support for my problems? Is the Bible true? Did I get brainwashed?
- Sometimes it is about sin: Some people think that when they become a Christian, they will stop sinning instantly. So when they do sin, they think that they haven't really become a Christian at all.
- Some people think that they "have not done it correctly". They wonder if they have said a proper prayer of commitment, or if they have done the right things to become a Christian.

What does "righteousness" mean?
One simple way to explain this is to say that being righteous means being "good enough for God", or having a "right standing with God". It is important to understand the difference between two kinds of righteousness:

1. **Jesus shares his righteousness with Christians.** Jesus is the only human who ever lived a truly righteous life. When you become a Christian, Christ gives you his righteousness. In other words, God looks at us and sees the goodness and purity of his Son. This means he can accept us, and so we are saved from the judgment of God.
2. **Christians try to live holy lives.** As we grow in our faith, we aim to live lives more like Jesus. We aim to be more holy, pure and righteous. But our righteousness can't save us. It is not the reason for our salvation, but it is the grateful response.

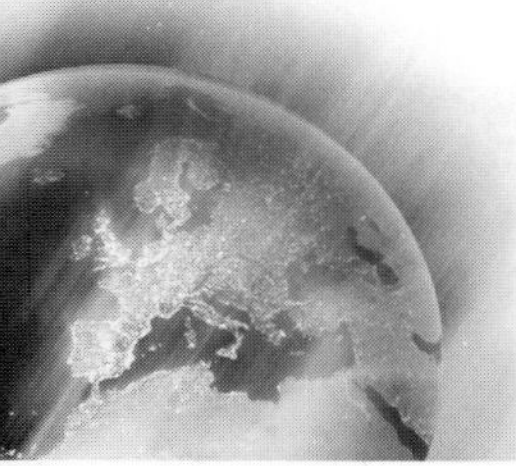

WEEK 2: PHILIPPIANS 1:12-26

What am I living for?

RECAP

Recap what we learned last week or ask the group to summarise what they learned last week. There may be someone who has just come to this study, and missed the last one. If needed, there is a short summary on page 9 of the Bible study booklet.

OPENING DISCUSSION QUESTION

Tell the group three things that make you happy.

The aim of this question is to get people talking about what brings them joy. You could try these alternatives, if you think they are more suitable for your group:

- ***Ask them to draw three things that make them happy, then talk about them to the others. You can have some fun looking at each other's drawings.***
- ***Ask people to think of a specific time they remember when they were especially happy.***
- ***Charades: ask them to act out something that makes them happy.***
- ***Name a piece of music that makes you happy.***

Read Philippians 1:12-26

If your group members have English as a second language, encourage them to read the passage a second time in their own language. This will help them to better understand the passage but it will also help them if and when they return home—see page 32.

There is a list of Bible words from this week's passage (NIV) on pages 10-11 of the Bible study booklet. Depending on your group, it may be appropriate to go through some or all of these words at this point. The word list for this study is shown over the page.

Leader's checklist

Have you...

- ☐ Reviewed how the first week went? Is there anything you want to change?
- ☐ Reminded people of the time and place where you will meet? (By phone, email or text.)
- ☐ Prepared food and drinks?
- ☐ Sufficient Bibles or printed out sheets with the Bible passages on them?
- ☐ The optional Discipleship Explored DVD ready to play?
- ☐ Printed out the daily study material (if you are going to use it)?
- ☐ Thought through your answers to each of the questions?
- ☐ Prayed for each group member and yourself?

Bible words

v12 brothers. Christians. All Christians are part of God's family.

v12 gospel. The message (good news) about Jesus Christ.

v12 advance the gospel. Help more people understand the message about Jesus.

v14 encouraged. Become more confident.

v14 courageously. Bravely.

v15 preach Christ. Explain who Christ is and what he has done for us on the cross; tell the gospel.

v15 envy. Wanting what belongs to other people.

v15 rivalry. Competing against other people because you want to be the best.

v16 the latter. The people mentioned second (in verse 15).

v17 the former. The people mentioned first (in verse 15).

v17 selfish ambition. Wanting to make yourself more important than other people. (Note: this definition is meant for this passage – you might need to explain that ambition can be positive as well.)

v17 sincerely. Honestly.

v18 motives. Reasons.

v18 I rejoice. I am joyful (very happy).

v19 The Spirit of Jesus Christ. The Holy Spirit. God sends his Holy Spirit to help people who become Christians.

v19 deliverance. Salvation (not rescue from prison, but being saved by God, from sin, death and judgment).

v20 eagerly. Very much.

v20 sufficient. Enough.

v20 exalted. Honoured.

v21 gain. Something better.

v22 fruitful labour. Hard work that gets good results.

v23 torn between. Can't decide between two things.

v23 depart. Leave.

v25 progress. Growth.

v25 the faith. Your relationship with God.

v26 on account of. Because of.

Read Philippians 1:12-18a

(1) ***What makes Paul happy (verse 18)? What is most important to him?***

Paul rejoices that Christ is being made known to other people. It is the most important thing in his life.

Follow-up questions

- ***Why do you think this is the most important thing for him?***

This is an opportunity for you to summarise the gospel message for your group. Our most important need is for forgiveness, because we are all sinners in God's sight, and deserve his judgment. Paul is filled with joy because he has been forgiven and saved by God. He wants other people to hear about the forgiveness that they can have through Christ.

Optional follow-up questions

(You may want to save the following question for later in the study.)

- ***What is the difference between happiness and the joy that Paul talks about?***

Happiness is something that depends on your circumstances. You feel happy because you have a new job, or because the sun is shining. Joy is much deeper. One way to understand the differences between joy and happiness is to think about their opposites. The opposite of happiness is unhappiness. But the opposite of joy is fear. Christians do not have to smile and be happy all the time. But we can experience joy even when bad things happen to us because we know that we are loved and accepted by God. Nothing can change that.

2 *Read verses 12-14 again. Where is Paul? Why is he there?*

He is in prison.

NIV uses the phrase "in chains". We don't know whether Paul was alone in a cell, or whether he was chained to a guard. This often happened to Roman prisoners (see for example Acts 12:6).

Why is he there? He has been imprisoned "for Christ" – probably meaning that he has been arrested for telling others about Jesus Christ.

3 *Many people think being in prison is a disaster. What does Paul think (see verses 12-14)?*

He is actually quite glad. **Why?** Because...

- **verse 12:** it has served to advance the gospel.
- **verse 13:** the whole palace guard has found out about Christ.
- **verse 14:** Christians have become more bold in telling other people about Jesus Christ. Note: You might think that the imprisonment of a Christian leader for preaching about Christ would have stopped the followers from speaking. The opposite is true. Inspired by Paul, they spoke more boldly about Christ.

4 *What surprises you about verses 15-18 and why?*

More people are preaching Christ! Some are doing so because they love and support Paul. Others are doing this to get Paul into more trouble! But Paul isn't worried about why others are preaching Christ. In fact, he's happy, because more people are hearing about Jesus Christ.

(5) *Have you, or someone you know, experienced opposition because you are a Christian?*

There may be a wide variety of answers to this question, for example being bullied or misunderstood by friends and family. Many new Christians have non-Christian partners, or unsympathetic families. If you have group members who are not believers yet, ask them: "What opposition do you think you might experience if you become a Christian?"

Note: *Listen carefully to the problems that your group mentions. Some of them may need private help and advice from you or your co-leaders.*

(6) *Paul experienced opposition because of his faith. How does Paul's example help us to think differently about the opposition we will face?*

Paul knows that the most important thing is that Christ is preached. This shapes how he thinks about everything. He can rejoice in prison because he knows that the good news about Jesus is spreading as a result.

Try to help your group to think about opposition in a similar way. For example, they may have been rejected by friends or family because they have accepted the gospel. But, their friends and family have heard about Christ from them. And this is the most important thing for them. Encourage them to continue talking about their faith in Christ respectfully to others, and to show their love and concern in practical ways.

Note: *Don't minimise the pain that some of your group may be feeling. We can have joy in our circumstances, but these things remain deeply upsetting.*

Read Philippians 1:18b-26

(7) *Who helps Paul (verse 19)?*

The Christians in Philippi (by praying for Paul) and the Spirit of Jesus Christ.

Follow-up question

- ***What does Paul mean by "the Spirit of Jesus Christ"?***

The Holy Spirit. Make sure your group understands who the Holy Spirit is:

- He is a person, not a thing or a force.
- He is God, together with the Father and the Son.
- He has the character and holiness of Jesus Christ.
- He is given as a gift to everyone who is a disciple of Jesus Christ.

8 *What does Paul think about his death? Why? (see verses 21-23)*

Note: *You may want to rephrase this question to ask: What is Paul's attitude to death? Why?*

- verses 21 & 23: Death is better than living!

Why? Because when Paul dies, he knows he will be gaining something. What he gains is explained in verse 23 – he will be with Christ forever!

Revelation 21:3-4 tells us that the future God has for us will be wonderful. Our relationship with him will no longer be spoiled by our sin. There will be no more death, mourning, crying or pain. That is why Paul sees death as something he gains from. This is the promise of the gospel.

9 *Why does Paul choose life instead of death (see verses 22-26)?*

- **verse 22:** While he is alive, he can do "fruitful labour" for Christ – he can serve God.
- **verse 24:** The Philippian Christians need his help – he does not want to leave them in need.
- **verses 25-26:** Paul can help them grow in the faith, and encourage them – they will be joyful in Christ as a result.

10 *How would your friends finish this sentence: "For me to live is..."?*

Ask your group to think about the most important things in the lives of their friends. This question is designed to help the group think about the difference that belonging to Christ makes. We no longer live for money, careers, comfort, or even our families – although all these things can be enjoyed as God's gifts to us. A disciple is learning how to live for Christ.

• *How would you finish the same sentence? "For me to live is..."?*

Let your group be real at this point and handle their answers lightly. Don't assume that they will answer like Paul! Being a disciple is about learning to live for Christ. Many of your group may only just be becoming aware of how much of a change being a Christian will mean for them. Like us, they may at times struggle to understand that Christ is more important than their families, partner, job etc.
For some of your group, the challenge of this study may be that they have not yet put their faith in Christ.

(11) *Paul says in verse 21: "To live is Christ and to die is gain". What does he mean?*

"To live is Christ" – A disciple is someone who is learning how to live for Christ. It means that everything we do should be because we want to see Jesus become better known and honoured by others. It is not just that living for Jesus is the most important thing in our lives. It means that living for Christ is the thing which underlies everything we do in life.

"To die is gain" – See leader's notes for question 8 above.

 *Optional follow-up discussion*

This might be a good moment to think again about the joys that were mentioned earlier, or the difficulties discussed by your group, and to think together about how our response is shaped by verse 21.
There are many things that we enjoy in this life. We need not feel guilty about enjoying them! They are God's gifts to us, and we should accept them with thanks and praise.

We will see many of our difficulties in life as unimportant compared to the big thing that is ours through Christ – eternity with him.

(12) *Look again at what Paul thinks about his own suffering – verses 12, 18a & 21. What does this teach us about praying for Christians who are suffering for the gospel?*

We need to pray for Christians who are facing opposition or persecution – both in our local area and in the wider world.
- Pray that their suffering will "advance the gospel" (verse 12)
- Pray that they will be able to rejoice as Paul did that Christ is being preached (verse 18a)
- Ask God to give them the strength to live for Christ and the faith to trust that death is "gain" (verse 21).

Note: *Remember that internationals in your group might return to situations of persecution.*

(13) *God does not promise us easy lives when we become Christians. What have we learned that will help us when we suffer for the gospel?*

Specific points might include:
- The most important thing is that Christ is made known to others.
- God helps us by his Holy Spirit.
- We are helped by other people praying for us.
- We can help other Christians by praying for them.

- We can be joyful even in difficult times.
- We can look forward to death because (for all who have put their trust in Christ) it is now the doorway to life.

This is a summary question for the study that aims to get the group thinking practically about what it will mean for them to live for Christ. Help people to be specific in their answers, ie: not "I must live for Christ this week" but "I must not worry about feeling uncomfortable when I tell others that I am a Christian".

MEMORY VERSE

"For to me, to live is Christ and to die is gain." Philippians 1:21. At the end of each session we have included a memory verse taken from the Bible passage the group has studied. You may find it helpful to read this together as you finish the session. Ask your group members to learn this verse during the week. If your group members have English as a second language, encourage them to learn the verse in their own language as well.

PRAY

Share with the rest of the group things you would like to pray for. Pray especially for those who are suffering for their faith. Pray they would know the confidence that Paul has.

Group members may find it helpful to write down something to pray for in the box on page 12 of the Bible study booklet. This will help those who are not used to praying aloud or who lack confidence.

DVD

If you feel it's appropriate for your group, you may want to show the *Discipleship Explored* DVD at this point. The DVD can be used as a summary or as a refresher for the main teaching point in this session.

DAILY BIBLE STUDIES

We have prepared some simple daily Bible-reading notes for you to use with the group, which reinforce some of the truths that have been learned at this session, and encourage them to start a daily discipline of Bible reading and prayer. The notes are available for download from www.discipleshipexplored.org

Group members will benefit from the model of having a daily time with God. But use these notes with discretion – they may be too much for some to attempt.

CONCLUSION

Finish by encouraging your group members to come back next week. Tell them: "This week, we've seen what it means to be living for Christ. Next week, we'll see that being a disciple is never something you can do on your own..."

Additional notes for leaders

Why is Paul content with people preaching Christ from false motives when he so clearly condemns false teachers in chapter 3? Paul's whole life is focused on knowing Christ and making him known. The fact that he is overjoyed at the preaching of Christ by these rivals shows that the gospel they are preaching must be the true one, even if they are doing so out of a personal hostility towards Paul. So the apostle does not really care if he is in prison, or that others have it in for him. He is overjoyed that the gospel is being heard.

There are two places in the Gospels where a similar question comes up. In Luke 9:49-50, Jesus says that the disciples are not to stop people who were casting out demons in his name. Here the principle is: "Whoever is not against us is for us". In this instance, Jesus is saying that what they are doing is not harmful, and brings glory to him, even though they are not part of the band of disciples.

But in Luke 11:23, Jesus says the opposite: "He who is not with me is against me." Here, Jesus is making the a point that salvation depends upon belonging to him. There are only two alternatives: belonging to the world of Satan, which will be destroyed, and belonging to the kingdom of God, where you will be saved.

What is "the help given by the Spirit of Jesus Christ"? The kind of help Paul received from the Holy Spirit is not explained, but we know from the rest of the Bible that God's Spirit helps us in many ways:

- The Holy Spirit changes us to become more like Jesus (Galatians 5:22-23).
- He helps us to pray (Romans 8:26-27).
- The Holy Spirit helps us to be bold in telling others the good news about Jesus Christ (Acts 4:31).
- He fills us with wisdom and understanding, so that we come to know God better and find out how He wants us to live (Colossians 1:9-10).

Note: You don't need to explain all this to your group today but it will help you to have thought about how to explain it.

Why does Paul say that dying is "gain"? We know from the resurrection of Jesus Christ that the future God has for us will be wonderful. No more sin in our lives. No more frustration from living in a world that has rejected God. Now we only understand Christ partly. When we die, we will be with him.

This is the promise of the gospel. Genuine Christianity is not about having a better life now – although Christ does that in many ways through giving us forgiveness, a new hope and a new family. Now, we experience in part – then we'll experience it fully.

Paul says that "to live is Christ and to die is gain". Why should we live for Christ? Is this realistic for Christians? If you have extra time, think about why a disciple tries to live his life for Christ:

- Jesus is the Lord – He deserves to be first.
- Jesus is our rescuer – He has bought our lives at the cost of His own life.
- Jesus is our future – He is the one who guarantees our eternal life.
- If we understand how much we have been forgiven, we will want to serve Christ out of love and thankfulness.

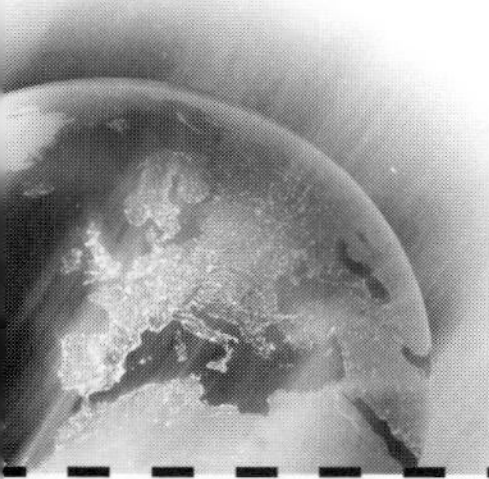

WEEK 3: PHILIPPIANS 1:27 – 2:11

Together for Christ?

RECAP

Recap what we learned last week or ask the group to summarise what they learned last week. If needed, there is a short summary on page 13 of the Bible study booklet.

OPENING DISCUSSION QUESTION

Talk about a team or group you have enjoyed being a member of.

*This question is designed to introduce the idea of partnership and fellowship (the Greek word for this is "*koinonia*"). Being a disciple of Jesus Christ is not a solitary occupation. We are saved to be part of God's family, and his design is that we should work together for the gospel. Encourage the group to talk about things they have done, either successes (or failures) on a sports team, or in clubs or societies.*

Follow-up question

- ***What did you enjoy about it?***

No need to comment on any of these, but there will be an opportunity to return to them later in the study.

Read aloud Philippians 1:27 – 2:11

If your group members have English as a second language, encourage them to read the passage a second time in their own language. This will help them to better understand the passage but it will also help them if and when they return home—see page 32.

Note: *There is a list of Bible words from this week's passage (NIV) on pages 14-15 of the Bible study booklet. Depending on your group,*

Leader's checklist

Have you…

- ☐ Reminded people of the time and place where you will meet? (By phone, email or text.)
- ☐ Prepared food and drinks?
- ☐ Sufficient Bibles or printed out sheets with the Bible passages on them?
- ☐ The optional Discipleship Explored DVD ready to play?
- ☐ Printed out the daily study material (if you are going to use it)?
- ☐ Thought through your answers to each of the questions?
- ☐ Prayed for each group member and yourself as the leader?

it may be appropriate to go through some or all of these words at this point. The word list for this study is shown below.

Bible words

v27 conduct. Behave.

v27 a manner. A way of doing or being.

v27 worthy. Honouring.

v27 in my absence. When I am not with you.

v27 contending. Struggling.

v27 oppose. Disagree with; try to stop.

v28 sign. Signal or symbol.

v29 granted. Given.

2v1 encouragement. Confidence, support, strength.

2v1 fellowship. Partnership.

2v1 tenderness and compassion. Kindness, love and concern.

2v3 selfish ambition. Wanting to be better than other people.

2v3 vain conceit. Stupid pride (pride = thinking you are better or more clever than others).

2v3 humility. The opposite of pride (see above).

2v5 attitude. Way of thinking or feeling (about something).

2v6 equality with. Being the same as.

2v6 grasped. Held on to.

2v7 the very nature of. The form of.

2v9 exalted. Raised up; lifted up and honoured.

2v11 every tongue. Every person.

2v11 confess. Say publicly.

Read Philippians 1:27-30

Paul is in prison, and unsure whether he will live or die. His situation is uncertain. But he writes to his friends to encourage them to keep going as disciples.

1 ***How does Paul want the Philippian Christians to behave (see verse 27a)?***

He says they should conduct themselves in a manner worthy of the gospel of Christ.

Follow-up question

- ***What do you think Paul means by this?***

They should live in a way that shows what the gospel is like – not just as individuals but also as a whole Christian community. The way they (and we) behave should point people towards the gospel and show what it means to be a Christian.

Optional follow-up question

- ***What kind of conduct dishonours the gospel? What kind of conduct honours the gospel?***

Over the next few weeks we will study the examples Paul gives the Philippians.

"To stand firm in one spirit" and "contend as one man for the faith of the gospel" (verse 27) means to stay sure of what they believe, and work together for the gospel.

2 ***Why was it important that the Philippians (and we) "stand firm in one spirit"?***

- There were people who opposed them (verse 28) and who wanted to see them fail. When they stood together in their faith, they proved that their faith was genuine.
- If they did not support and encourage each other, they might have been tempted to give up. If people give up their faith, other people might doubt the gospel.
- They need each other's courage and determination as an example.

3 ***Why was it important that they (and we) "contend as one man for the faith of the gospel"?***

Note: *The phrase "contend as one man" is best explained with an example. Paul probably had a group of foot soldiers in mind – standing close together, fighting as one unit.*

- Although there were many Christians in Philippi, they needed to be united and stand together against the opposition they faced as they told people about Jesus.
- The Philippians were struggling together to tell people about Jesus. It was not easy, so they needed each other's support and encouragement. They needed to keep reminding each other of the truth of the gospel and why they needed to tell others the gospel message.
- Being a Christian is a "team sport"! We should work together and encourage one another to stand firm in the Christian life and to tell others about Jesus Christ. It's more like playing soccer than playing chess.

4 ***Paul and the Philippian church faced opposition because they were "contending", or fighting, for the gospel (verse 28-30). Why do you think the gospel causes opposition?***

There are many reasons why people oppose the gospel message:

- In Philippi, Paul faced opposition because the gospel brought change that some people didn't like. (See the story of the slave girl in Philippi in Acts 16:16-24.)
- The gospel challenges our allegiances or loyalties. Jesus demands that following him should be our number one priority. Obeying Jesus is even more important

than obeying our parents, boss or government. When someone becomes a Christian, this can cause tension. This is especially true when people have converted from another religion, or where they come from a group-orientated culture where becoming a Christian may be seen as rejecting the family (see Luke 14:26, 33). In cultures influenced by Confucius, loyalty to your parents is one of the most important priorities in life. In Muslim cultures, someone who becomes a Christian is likely to be rejected or even killed.

- Jesus claims to be "the only way". This is very offensive to people who think "all religions are equal".
- Some people just hate religion in general.

5 *What advice does Paul give the Philippians (and us) to help them as they face opposition?*

- Always conduct yourself in a manner worthy of the gospel.
- Be united – stick together with other Christians.
- Be part of a fellowship of believers where you can be encouraged.
- Don't be afraid.

Optional follow-up question

- ***Who helped Paul when he faced opposition?***

The Philippian Christians (by praying for Paul) and the Holy Spirit (1:19).

6 *Sometimes people say that if you become a Christian, you will be wealthy and healthy. What does Paul teach in verses 29-30 about the Christian life?*

- Suffering is normal for Christians.
- Faith in Christ is a gift. Suffering for Christ is a gift too (verse 29).
- If we expect the Christian life to be easy, we will be disappointed – because it is not!

Note: *Nobody who saw the life of Christ (see 2:6-11) could think that Christians should expect to be wealthy and healthy. Jesus died with nothing.*

Read Philippians 2:1-11

7 ***Paul uses the word "if" four times in verse 1. What four things should make the Philippians "one in spirit and purpose"?***

- **"Encouragement from being united with Christ".** We are united to Jesus. He lives in us by his Holy Spirit.
- **"Comfort from his love".** God has shown us great love in sending Jesus Christ into the world to die for us. This love should comfort us when things go wrong or if we feel lost, lonely or guilty. See Romans 8:28-39.
- **"Fellowship with the Spirit".** This primarily refers to the way that the Holy Spirit helps us have fellowship with other believers. The Spirit gives us love for other Christians, helps us see we're part of the same family, and helps us want to work together for the gospel. See Philippians 1:27.
- **"Tenderness and compassion".** Jesus Christ is full of love and mercy towards others. Those who belong to him start to have these same attitudes towards others.

8 ***Read verses 3 & 4. How should Christians treat each other if they are one in spirit and purpose?***

With kindness and generosity:

- Not being selfish
- Not putting themselves or their ambitions first

With humility:

- Not looking for glory or praise for themselves
- Considering others better than themselves
- Putting other people's needs or interests first

What stops us from doing this?

- Selfish ambition or vain conceit
- Thinking we are better than other people
- Putting our own interests first

Growing as a disciple of Jesus doesn't happen automatically. God has started a good work in us, but we must fight our selfishness and sin. Growing as a Christian is a fight against our own pride.

9 *If you "look to the interests of others", what will you do?*

Encourage your group members to give very practical answers and to consider different situations. E.g.

- In this Bible-study group
- In their family
- With their friends
- At church

10 *Whose example should we be following (verse 5)? Why?*

Jesus' example! Being a disciple means being a follower of Jesus. We should be growing like him in his love, humility, compassion, and willingness to be our servant. Jesus loved us so much that he was willing to suffer and die for us. If we are following him, we must give up our pride and be willing to serve him and others in the same way.

MEMORY VERSE

"Your attitude should be the same as that of Christ Jesus." Philippians 2:5.
At the end of each session we have included a memory verse taken from the Bible passage the group has studied. You may find it helpful to read this together as you finish the session. Ask your group members to learn this verse during the week. If your group members have English as a second language, encourage them to learn the verse in their own language as well.

PRAY

Read Philippians 2:1-11 again. Use these verses to help you to pray.

If the members of your group still find it difficult to pray aloud, suggest that they each choose a verse or short phrase from Philippians 2:1-11. They can read this verse out and then thank God for this truth from the Bible.

If the group came up with practical answers to question 9, encourage them to turn these into prayers, as they ask God to help them to become more like Jesus and look to the interests of others.

DVD

If you feel it's appropriate for your group, you may want to show the *Discipleship Explored* DVD at this point. The DVD can be used as a summary or as a refresher for the main teaching point in this session.

DAILY BIBLE STUDIES

We have prepared some simple daily Bible-reading notes for you to use with the group, which reinforce some of the truths that have been learned at this session, and encourage them to start a daily discipline of Bible reading and prayer. The notes are available for download from www.discipleshipexplored.org

Group members will benefit from the model of having a daily time with God. But use these notes with discretion – they may be too much for some to attempt.

CONCLUSION

Finish by encouraging your group members to come back next week. Tell them: "This week, we've seen that being a disciple is about being part of God's family. Next week, we will look in more detail at one of the most wonderful parts of the Bible…"

Additional notes for leaders

How does "Whatever happens, conduct yourselves in a manner worthy of the gospel of Christ.", link with the whole passage of 1:27 – 2:11? This opening sentence gives the structure of what follows in the rest of the today's passage (1:27 – 2:11). Paul tells them what they should be doing (1:27 – 2:4) and how they should be doing it (2:1-11).

How can I explain "stand firm in one spirit"? You might find it helpful to use this illustration: Explain that when a lump of coal drops out of a fire or a barbeque, it quickly becomes cold. It only burns and gives off heat when it is in the fire with other pieces of coal. It's the same with Christians. When we are part of a fellowship of believers, encouraging each other and working together, we will work well as disciples. When we stay away and try to do it on our own, we will quickly go cold. We need to look after each other, and try to give the fellowship and encouragement our Christian brothers and sisters need, if they can't meet with others because of illness, travel, or other family commitments.

What is the "sign to them that they will be destroyed, but that you will be saved"? What is this sign? When disciples stick together and support one another in their work for the gospel, it is a sign that they genuinely belong to Christ. It is part of the "fruit of righteousness" (1:11). It is one of the outward signs of the inner change that God is at work in you. It is a sign that you will be saved by God on the day of Christ (1:6, 10) – when everyone in the world will be judged. If someone is opposed to believers, this shows that they are not in Christ. Therefore they will not be saved, but destroyed. This is how Paul himself once was – persecuting Christians! But God saved even him – "the worst of sinners" (1 Timothy 1:15-16).

What does it mean to be "in Christ"? One of Paul's definitions of what it means to be a Christian is that we are "in Christ". This phrase appears a lot in Philippians. We are united to Jesus. Sometimes we talk about Jesus living in us – you may have prayed a prayer to "invite Jesus into your heart". This is true. He lives in us by his Holy Spirit. But the bigger truth is that we live in him. We are "in him" so that we can escape the wrath of God – because God sees the righteousness of Christ rather than our sinfulness. We can be called sons of God, because we are in him – the Son of God. We have eternal security, because we are in Christ – who is now seated in heaven. You might ask your group members: "Does the understanding that you are in Christ excite you?" If yes, then this would be a sign that God had started his work in them. See Ephesians 2.

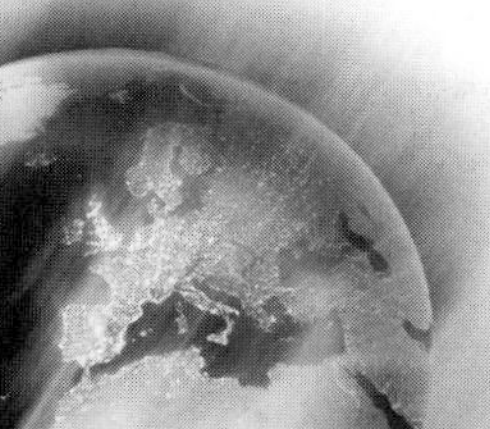

WEEK 4: PHILIPPIANS 2:5-18

How should I live for Christ?

RECAP

Recap what we learned last week or ask the group to summarise what they learned last week. If needed, there is a short summary on page 17 of the Bible study booklet.

OPENING DISCUSSION QUESTION

Which do you think is more important? To tell people the gospel or to live a godly life? Why?

Give the members of the group time to share their answers, but don't try to come to any final conclusion. The answer to this question will become clear as we study this passage.

Read aloud Philippians 2:5-18

If your group members have English as a second language, encourage them to read the passage a second time in their own language. This will help them to better understand the passage but it will also help them if and when they return home—see page 32.

There is a list of Bible words from this week's passage (NIV) on pages 18-19 of the Bible study booklet. Depending on your group, it may be appropriate to go through some or all of these words at this point. The word list for this study is shown over the page.

Leader's checklist

Have you...

- [ ] Reminded people of the time and place where you will meet? (By phone, email or text.)
- [ ] Prepared food and drinks?
- [ ] Sufficient Bibles or printed out sheets with the Bible passages on them?
- [ ] The optional Discipleship Explored DVD ready to play?
- [ ] Printed out the daily study material (if you are going to use it)?
- [ ] Thought through your answers to each of the questions?
- [ ] Prayed for each group member and yourself as the leader?

Bible words

v5 attitude. Way of thinking or feeling (about something).

v6 equality with. Being the same as.

v6 grasped. Held on to.

v7 the very nature of. The form of.

v9 exalted. Raised up; lifted up and honoured.

v11 every tongue. Every person.

v11 confess. Say publicly.

v12 in my presence. When I am with you.

v12 trembling. Shaking because you are afraid.

v15 blameless and pure. Someone who does not think wrong things or do wrong things.

v15 without fault. Without anything wrong.

v15 crooked and depraved. Sinful and evil.

v16 the word of life. The message about Jesus (the gospel).

v16 boast. Gladly tell everyone.

v16 the day of Christ. The day when Jesus Christ will return to judge the world.

v16 run or labour. Work hard.

v17 drink offering. A drink offering = an Old Testament offering (a gift to God) of wine or water.

v17 sacrifice. An offering to God. Chosen animals were sacrificed (killed as a gift to God). Sometimes in the Old Testament, a drink offering was poured on top of the sacrifice.

Read Philippians 2:5-11

Paul is telling his readers how they should live as disciples, following the example of Jesus.

1 ***What do verses 6-7 tell us about the identity of Jesus – who is he?***

- **verse 6:** God – Jesus is, and has always been, fully God.
- **verse 7:** Human – Jesus became fully human.
- **verse 7:** Servant – Even though he is God, Jesus came to serve (Matthew 20:28).

Follow-up question

- ***Why is it important to understand this?***

i.e. Would it matter if Jesus was God and not a human being?
Yes. If Jesus was not a human being, he could not pay the price for our sin.
Would it matter if Jesus was only a man?
Yes, because:

- no human being is able to live a life free from sin;
- we needed someone who had no sin to pay the penalty for our sin;
- only God could live a life free from sin;
- only God has the authority to forgive sin because it is an offence against him.

2 *Verses 8 tells us that Jesus humbled himself. How did he humble himself?*

- **He became a man.** The one who has always existed, the creator of the universe, the all-powerful, all-knowing one – Jesus, who was fully God – became a human being.
- **He became a servant.** The Son holds a position of privilege and authority. A servant (or slave as it could be translated) holds the lowest position, without privilege, without power, under authority. When Jesus became the servant, he willingly gave up what was his by right in order to serve us.
- **He died on a cross.** Jesus made the ultimate sacrifice on our behalf. He gave up his life so that we could live. This is the ultimate expression of 2:3-4; considering others better than yourself and looking out for the interests of others. Jesus died a criminal's death when he had never sinned. The cross was the worst imaginable death you could die.

Follow-up question

- ***Why do you think Jesus did this?***

He knew it was the only way to save us. He loved us and put saving us as his top priority. So even though it meant giving up everything, he was willing to do it so that we could be forgiven and have a right relationship with the Father again.

Jesus' death on a cross was not the end. Three days later God brought Jesus back to life.

3 *What happened after Jesus came back to life (verse 9)?*

- God exalted Jesus to the highest place.
- God gave Jesus the name that is above every name.

- ***What will happen as the result of this (verses 10-11)?***

Verses 10-11 point forward to the time when Jesus will return and this world will come to an end. At that time, every knee will bow and every tongue confess that Jesus is Lord.

4 *Verses 5-11 show Jesus both as God and as our Servant King. He chose to be born as a human being so that he could die on the cross in our place.*

- ***How does this make you feel?***

Verses 5-11 are a wonderful summary of who Jesus is and what he did for us. Help the group to express some of the emotions that are natural when we understand the facts of the gospel – the amazing love and grace of Jesus towards us. Answers might include:

- We feel humbled – by his love for us.
- We feel thankful to Jesus for what he did for us.
- We are full of joy because Jesus has saved us.

• How should we respond? (See verse 5.)

- We should show the same attitude as Jesus.
- We should love and serve him for what he did for us.
- We should not ignore the great service he did for us by thinking we can get to God by our own efforts.

Note: *It may be appropriate to stop the group at this point, and encourage people to say prayers of thanks and praise to God our Father and the Lord Jesus Christ for their great love for us.*

Read Philippians 2:12-13

We have seen that when you become a Christian, God starts to change you on the inside. This inside change is shown by outside changes in our lives.

5 What does Paul tell the Philippian Christians to do in verse 12?

"Work out your salvation with fear and trembling."

• Why do you think Paul describes this as continuing to "work out your salvation"?

We need to keep working to make sure that we live like a person who has been saved by God. These "outside changes" will involve our hard work.

Make sure your group understands that this does not mean working **for** our salvation. Christ has already done all that is needed to save us. Once we are saved, our salvation will begin to work itself out in our lives in many ways.

- You may find it helpful to use the house illustration: when you move to a new house, there is an actual moving-in day. But then there is plenty of on-going work to get on with, as you change your house to become more and more like the home you want it to be.

⑥ *Why must we do this with "fear and trembling"?*

We must remember who God is. He is our creator and ruler. He is all-powerful and holy. Therefore we should be serious about how we relate to him. Proverbs 1:7 says that "The fear of the Lord is the beginning of knowledge". Of course, we also need to remember that God is our loving Father, who we can come to at any time with our needs.

⑦ *Look at verse 13. What is God doing while we are working out our salvation? How does that make you feel?*

God works in us to make us grow more and more like his Son Jesus. Just as children grow to look like their parents, so, when we become children of God, he helps us grow to be more like Jesus.

This should make us feel encouraged and confident. If it depended on us, we would fail!

Read Philippians 2:14-18

⑧ *Earlier in his letter Paul encouraged us to "conduct yourselves in a manner worthy of the gospel of Christ" (Philippians 1:27). In 2:14-16 what kind of behaviour is worthy of the gospel?*

- **not complaining** – since we already have everything we need because of Jesus, we should be noticeably different to those around us by not complaining about our circumstances, whatever they are.
- **not arguing** – again this is an opportunity to behave differently to those around us, as we show the same humility that Jesus had (2:3, 8).
- **blameless and pure** – not doing, saying or thinking wrong things.
- **holding out the word of life** – telling others the gospel message about Jesus.

⑨ *How should we "shine like stars"? Why?*

If we consider others better than ourselves (verse 3), look to the interests of others (verse 4), do everything without complaining or arguing (verse 14) and are blameless and pure, without fault (verse 15), then we will certainly be noticed by those around us! If our attitude is like Jesus (verse 5), then it will draw the attention of others – not so that they can then praise how amazing we are, but so that we can point them to the truth about Jesus as we tell them the gospel message.

(10) *Discuss the opening question again: Which do you think is more important – to tell people the gospel or to live a godly life among them? How does today's passage help you to answer this question?*

Both are important. Paul has given us an example to follow – the Lord Jesus (verses 5-11) – and very practical directions on how to live as a disciple (verses 2-4, 14-16). Living this kind of godly life will back up the gospel message we share with others, and may give us opportunities to share the gospel that we would not otherwise have – but it must not be seen as an alternative to telling people about Jesus.

MEMORY VERSE

"Shine like stars in the universe as you hold out the word of life."
Philippians 2:15-16. At the end of each session we have included a memory verse taken from the Bible passage the group has studied. You may find it helpful to read this together as you finish the session. Ask your group members to learn this verse during the week. If your group members have English as a second language, encourage them to learn the verse in their own language as well.

PRAY

Pray for each other, asking God to change you to become more and more like Jesus, shining like stars among your family, friends and community.

DVD

If you feel it's appropriate for your group, you may want to show the *Discipleship Explored* DVD at this point. The DVD can be used as a summary or as a refresher for the main teaching point in this session.

DAILY BIBLE STUDIES

We have prepared some simple daily Bible-reading notes for you to use with the group, which reinforce some of the truths that have been learned at this session, and encourage them to start a daily discipline of Bible reading and prayer. The notes are available for download from www.discipleshipexplored.org

Group members will benefit from the model of having a daily time with God. But use these notes with discretion – they may be too much for some to attempt.

CONCLUSION

Finish by encouraging your group members to come back next week. Tell them: "This week, we've seen what it means to follow the Lord Jesus as a humble servant. Next week, we'll find out the greatest threat to us as new Christians."

EXTRA BIBLE STUDY

In Philippians 2:19-30 Paul gives two examples of people who were living for Christ in the way he has been writing about. Timothy worked with Paul and had a deep concern for the Philippian Christians. Epaphroditus had travelled from Philippi to help Paul and to bring him gifts from the Philippians. There is a short additional Bible study about these two men on pages 37-38 of the Study Guide. There are a number of ways in which you might choose to use this extra study. These are explained on page 22 of this Leader's Guide. You will find Leader's Notes on the extra study on page 107.

Additional notes for leaders

Are there other places in the Bible where this image of humility is shown? John 13, where Jesus washes his disciples' feet, is an acted out example of what Paul tells us in Philippians 2:5-11. Jesus is fully God (John 13:3), but he takes on the nature of a servant (John 13:4-5). After washing their feet, Jesus returns to his place (John 13:12) and then tells his disciples that this is an example for them to follow (John 13:15).

How can I use 2:5-11 as an opportunity to summarise the gospel? How Jesus' death on the cross saves us is not explained in 2:5-11, but it gives a great opportunity to go over this if your group are not yet clear on the gospel.

If you have led this group for a while, you may have already used a way of summarizing what Jesus did on the cross – in which case, use that way again.

If not, one quick way to explain the gospel is to use the **Book illustration:**

Use any book (except a Bible, because the book stands for our sin!). Hold up your right hand. Explain that your hand represents you, and that the ceiling stands for God. Show the book, and ask them to imagine that it contains a record of your sin – every time you have done, said or thought things that are wrong. Put the book flat on your right hand. Ask: "What does the book do?" It separates you from God. This is a picture of what sin does. It gets in the way between us and God, and stops us knowing him as our friend. Now hold up your left hand. This stands for Jesus. Explain that Jesus lived a perfect life. He never sinned. There was nothing separating Jesus from God. Explain that as Jesus died on the cross, the sin of the whole world was put onto him. Transfer the book from your right hand to your left hand to show this. Ask: "What is there between Jesus and God?" This is why Jesus died – to take the punishment for all our sin. Now look back at your right hand: Ask: "What is there between me and God?" The answer is – nothing! When Jesus died on the cross, he took the punishment for our sins so that we can be forgiven. This means that there is nothing to separate us from God any more.

What does Paul mean by" a drink offering on the sacrifice"? If your group members ask about the meaning of verse 17, explain that a drink offering is an Old Testament offering (a gift to God) of wine or water. Sometimes in the Old Testament, when animals were sacrificed (killed as a gift to God), a drink offering was poured on top of the sacrifice. Paul is saying that the faith of these Christians and their work for the Lord is like an Old Testament sacrifice. Paul might have to die for the gospel. If this happens, it will be like a drink offering. His life will be given to God with the sacrifice (the faith and work) of the Philippian Christians.

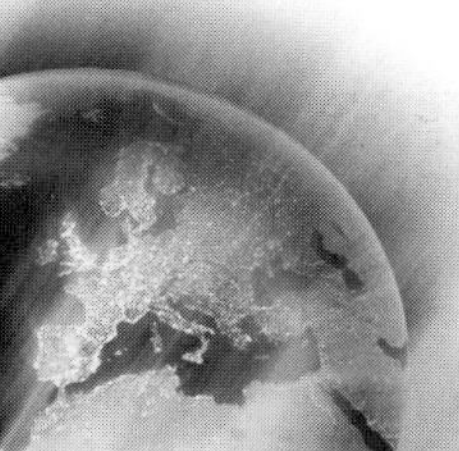

WEEK 5: PHILIPPIANS 3:1-9

Can I be good enough for God?

RECAP

Recap what we learned last week or ask the group to summarise what they learned last week. If needed, there is a short summary on page 21 of the Bible study booklet.

OPENING DISCUSSION QUESTION

What do people today think will make them good enough for God?

Answers to this will reflect the culture and religious background that the people come from. Possible areas to include may be:

Morality: doing good

Intentions: being sincere

Religion: belonging to the 'right' church, sect or religion. Doing their religious duty. Having been through a religious ritual like baptism, confirmation, been on a pilgrimage (Lourdes, Mecca). Coming from a religious family.

Religious experience: Having had an experience of healing, peace, closeness to God, 'enlightenment' etc.

Read aloud Philippians 3:1-9

If your group members have English as a second language, encourage them to read the passage a second time in their own language. This will help them to better understand the passage but it will also help them if and when they return home—see page 32.

There is a list of Bible words from this week's passage (NIV) on pages 22-23 of the Bible study booklet. Depending on your group, it may be appropriate to go through some or all of these words at this point. The word list for this study is shown over the page.

Leader's checklist

Have you...

- [ ] Reminded people of the time and place where you will meet? (By phone, email or text.)
- [ ] Prepared food and drinks?
- [ ] Sufficient Bibles or printed out sheets with the Bible passages on them?
- [ ] The optional Discipleship Explored DVD ready to play?
- [ ] Printed out the daily study material (if you are going to use it)?
- [ ] Thought through your answers to each of the questions?
- [ ] Prayed for each group member and yourself as the leader?

Bible words

v1 safeguard for you. A way to keep you safe.

v2 mutilators of the flesh. Those people who practise circumcision (see below) in order to get right with God.

v3 circumcision. Cutting off a small piece of skin from the penis. For Jewish people, circumcision is an outward sign showing that the man belongs to God's people. But God sent Jesus so that both Jews and non-Jews can become his people. Now the sign that someone is one of God's people is faith in Jesus and the Holy Spirit in their life, not physical circumcision.

v3 put no confidence in the flesh. Do not trust in things we do (like circumcision) to make us right with God.

v5 on the eighth day. At eight days old.

v5 tribe of Benjamin. All Jews came from one of 12 tribes (family groups). Benjamin was one of only two tribes that kept following God.

v5 Hebrew. Another word for Jew.

v5 Pharisee. A group of Jews who followed religious rules and customs very strictly.

v6 zeal. Enthusiasm or passion for a belief or idea.

v6 persecuting. Oppressing, treating badly.

v6 legalistic righteousness. Keeping the Law of Moses.

v8 surpassing. Exceptional, extraordinary.

v8-9 gain Christ and be found in him. Know Christ and belong to him.

Read Philippians 3:1-3

(1) ***From the outside, the situation looked bad for the Philippian Christians. Look back over chapters 1 & 2. What difficulties were the Philippians facing?***

- Paul was in prison (1:12-14).
- They were facing opposition and suffering for Christ (1:28-30).
- They were living in a "crooked and depraved generation" (2:14).

Even though the Philippians were facing opposition, Paul tells them to rejoice!

(2) ***From what we have already seen in Paul's letter, why should they rejoice?***

- Notice that they should rejoice not in what has happened – but "in the Lord" (verse 1), that is, in Jesus Christ.

Earlier Paul has said that they should rejoice because:

- God has begun a good work in them that he will complete (1:6).
- the gospel has been advanced by Paul's imprisonment (1:13-14, 17-18).
- we have a great future waiting for us as Christians (1:21, 23).
- of the love and unity we have in Christ (2:1-2).
- Jesus came to serve and save us (2:5-8).
- Jesus is Lord (2:9-11).
- God is working in us for his good purposes (2:13).

3 ***Rejoicing in all that Christ had done for them would protect them from another problem. What danger did they face (verses 2-3)?***

False teaching. **What was the false teaching?** Use the word definitions for "mutilators of the flesh" and "circumcision" to help the group work out what the problem was.

This will need some explanation. Paul is warning them about religious Jews who were trying to convince the Christians that they needed to follow some Old Testament laws in order to be saved. A sign that a man belonged to God's people in the Old Testament was that he was circumcised – had the foreskin cut off his penis. This outward, physical sign becomes a kind of shorthand word for "acceptable to God". Paul says that Christians are "the circumcision" (verse 3); that is, they are acceptable to God through Christ, even though they may not have had their foreskins cut off!

Some Jews were saying that you have to add something else to faith in Jesus in order to be right with God. In their case, it was Jesus plus Jewish laws.

• ***How will rejoicing in the Lord protect us from false teaching?***

We are protected from false teaching if we rejoice in what Christ has done for us. This means that if we know the gospel, and are thankful for it, we will not want to listen to false teaching.

4 ***What three things show that someone truly belongs to Christ (v 3)?***

- **They worship by the Spirit of God:** the whole of their lives are directed by the Holy Spirit.
- **They glory in Christ Jesus:** Christians rejoice in Jesus and all that he has done for them.
- **They put no confidence in the flesh:** Encourage your group to use the Bible words list to see what this phrase means. Christians don't rely on anything they have done to put them right with God. Some may object that they have done something: put their faith in Jesus. Remind them that even faith is a gift from God (Ephesians 2:8).

Read Philippians 3:4-9

5 ***Paul tells us how good he was as a religious Jew. What evidence does he give?***

He kept the Jewish law faultlessly (verse 6).
Go through Paul's list with your group, asking them what each of the following means:

- circumcised: cutting off a small piece of skin from the penis. See the Bible words list for a full explanation.
- on the eighth day: Jewish baby boys were circumcised at eight days old.
- of the people of Israel: in the Old Testament, the Jews were called Israelites.
- of the tribe of Benjamin: One of the 12 tribes of Israel. See the Bible words list for a full explanation.
- a Hebrew of Hebrews: a true Jew.
- a Pharisee: The Pharisees were a group of Jews who followed religious rules and customs very strictly.
- persecuting the church: before Paul became a Christian, he made trouble for the Christian church (Acts 9:1-2).

6 *What does Paul think about his religious background and efforts? Do you find that surprising?*

He had thought it was a huge benefit or 'gain' to be born a Jew and to keep the law. He now sees that it is actually worthless, or a load of rubbish.

Be careful to help your group understand what is meant by the word "religion". Make the point that true Christianity is not about the rules, traditions, ceremonies and structures of religion. It is about a relationship with the living God through Jesus Christ. Even Christianity can be turned into a "religion". But no good works of any kind lead to a relationship with God. However, finding a relationship with God through Christ leads to good works that please God. See Ephesians 2:8-10.

It is also important to help your group see that Paul is not saying one way is "better" than the other. Paul is passionate about his old way being of no use at all. This is surprising to us, because we often think that God is pleased with religion of any kind. In fact, God hates empty religion, because it is not the way to find forgiveness. Christ is the only way to forgiveness.

Your group may have given some examples from the opening question that you could pick up on here. Make the point that however impressive someone's religious status is, it does not get them any closer to God. Only Christ can do that.

Paul knows that keeping religious rules will never make people good enough for God. It is not just useless – it is also harmful.

7 *What makes us right with God?*

A righteousness that comes from God and is by faith in Christ (verse 9).

❓ Follow-up question

- ***What does not make us right with God?***

A righteousness of my own that comes from keeping the law (verse 9).

Notice that this comes from ourselves; the first comes from God.

❓ Optional follow-up exercise

These are two competing ways of knowing God – through Christ or through empty religion. Depending on your group, they might find it helpful to draw up a table:

What makes us right with God?	***What does not make us right with God?***
Christ	***Empty religion***
Trusting Jesus' death on the cross	Keeping rules
From God	From ourselves
Confident in Christ	Confident in ourselves
Leads to humility	Leads to pride
Glorious!	Rubbish
Does work	Doesn't work!

(8) *Why do you think Paul uses such insulting language: "dogs" (verse 2), "rubbish" (verse 8)?*

Empty religion is worse than useless – it is totally harmful. No religious activity will get you right with God. The problem is that doing religious things can make people think they are right with God when they are not. Doing religious things might even stop us from discovering that it is faith in Jesus that makes us right with God. Even the good things we do are rubbish when it comes to getting right with God. We can never do enough to be accepted by God.

Note: There may be some serious pastoral issues that group members have with this, particularly if they have family or friends who believe that keeping religious rules makes them right with God. New Christians need to be wise in knowing when and how to challenge the false religions and views of their families. Encourage new Christians to show their family and friends how they have changed, and to pray for opportunities to explain why they have changed when they are asked. (1 Peter 3:15)

(9) *Before you became a Christian, what things did you rely on to make you right with God?*

If your group struggle to answer this, be ready to share something from your own life. There are lots of possible answers to this, depending on the background and culture of the various members of your group. Some may have trusted in a religious system. Others may not have thought about God at all. Help these people see that even though they were not "religious" in any formal sense, their sense of being "OK" was built on something. That is what they needed to stop relying on. E.g. money or "I was a kind person with lots of gifts and talents".

(10) *What things can you be tempted to rely on, in addition to your faith in Jesus?*

It is unlikely that your group will find themselves facing the problem of circumcision, but there are other kinds of "Jesus Plus" teaching today:

• Baptism. Some people will say that you have to be baptised in a certain way to be properly Christian. It is a good thing to be baptised as a sign of your new relationship with God in Christ, but baptism is not what makes you a Christian.

• Speaking in tongues. Some Christians will say that you must have a special experience of being filled with the Holy Spirit and speaking in other languages before you can be considered to be a "real" Christian. This is not true.

• Belonging to a certain church. Some Christians think that only their denomination or church is the "true church". This is wrong. The true church is everyone who is right with God by faith in Christ (all Christians are "saints" as Paul says in 1:1).

Members of your group may come up with some other examples, which might need to be handled with care.

(11) *Imagine you have a friend who tells you that they are not good enough for God. What would you say to them?*

Your group members will find it helpful to explain things in their own words. Their answers to this question will also help you to check whether your group have understood the main teaching from this session.

(12) *How can we help each other to keep trusting in Jesus, and not to trust in anything else?*

Try to encourage practical answers to this question, so that members of the group can give each other ongoing help and encouragement. Answers could include:

- "Rejoice in the Lord" (3:1). Discuss ways to help each other to rejoice, both when meeting with other Christians and also when on your own.

- Remind each other of the truth of the gospel message – that Jesus Christ has done everything that's needed for us to be right with God.
- Encourage each other to read the Bible and pray regularly – not as a way to "get right with God", but to help you get to know God better and better.
- Encourage each other to keep meeting with other Christians regularly. Perhaps members of the group could agree to look after each other and to contact anyone who is missing from a group meeting or church service. This kind of "accountability" can be really helpful in supporting someone who is finding it hard to keep up a regular habit of meeting with other Christians. It also means that others in the group will quickly find out if someone is ill or has some kind of problem that is preventing them from coming.

MEMORY VERSE

"Not having a righteousness of my own that comes from the law, but that which is through faith in Christ – the righteousness that comes from God and is by faith." Philippians 3:9. At the end of each session we have included a memory verse taken from the Bible passage the group has studied. You may find it helpful to read this together as you finish the session. Ask your group members to learn this verse during the week. If your group members have English as a second language, encourage them to learn the verse in their own language as well.

PRAY

- Praise God that Jesus saves you when keeping religious rules can't.
- Pray that you will rejoice in the gospel.
- Pray that you will be alert for those who try to add things to the gospel.
- Pray for anyone in your group whose family or friends believe that keeping religious rules makes them good enough for God.

DVD

If you feel it's appropriate for your group, you may want to show the *Discipleship Explored* DVD at this point. The DVD can be used as a summary or as a refresher for the main teaching point in this session.

DAILY BIBLE STUDIES

We have prepared some simple daily Bible-reading notes for you to use with the group, which reinforce some of the truths that have been learned at this session, and encourage them to start a daily discipline of Bible reading and prayer. The notes are available for download from www.discipleshipexplored.org

Group members will benefit from the model of having a daily time with God. But use these notes with discretion – they may be too much for some to attempt.

CONCLUSION

Finish by encouraging your group members to come back next week. Tell them: "This week we have seen the big threat that false religion is to our faith in Christ. Next week, we'll see how we can stand firm as disciples of Christ."

Additional notes for leaders

Why is something that God originally gave – the law and the Jewish religion – now rubbish? This is a complex issue that is dealt with in depth in Romans 1-11. For now, make the point that the Old Testament law was never meant to be a way of getting right with God, but rather a temporary picture to teach his people how Christ would save us.

Jesus does not abolish the Old Testament; but he does fulfil every bit of it. And he fulfils different parts of it in different ways. For example:

- Sacrifices are no longer necessary, because Jesus is the final sacrifice.
- Food laws are no longer necessary, because Jesus' people are to show they are different by their purity and how they love one another, not by the foods they eat. We do not need to keep the law, because Jesus perfectly kept the law for us.
- By contrast, Jesus deepens the moral requirements of the law – it is not just the act of murder which is wrong, but being angry with your brother. It is not just adultery which is wrong, but lust and impure thoughts.

The key point to make clear is that the Old Testament law is good when it is used for what it was intended for: to show people their need for Christ's sacrifice. When people treat it as a way of salvation, it becomes worse than useless. It is dangerous and a lie.

This is why Paul used such insulting language about those who taught this. They said that people could be saved by works of religion, and this is wrong. Only Christ can save.

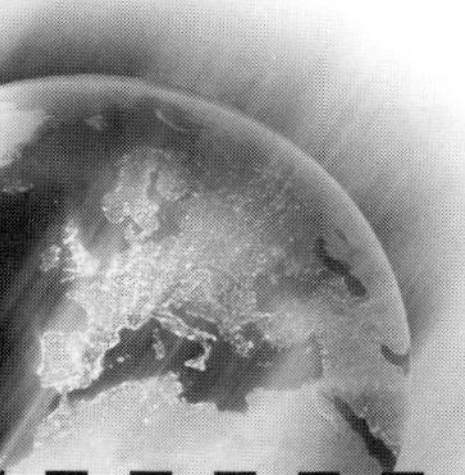

WEEK 6: PHILIPPIANS 3:10 – 4:1

How can I know Christ better?

RECAP

Recap what we learned last week or ask the group to summarise what they learned last week. If needed, there is a short summary on page 25 of the Bible study booklet.

OPENING DISCUSSION QUESTION

What is the difference between knowing about someone and knowing them as a friend? List some ways you can get to know someone better.

This question is designed to get people thinking about how relationships and knowledge about a person are achieved. Try and keep the discussion short and light-hearted.

It is worth thinking about two different kinds of "knowing". We can know a lot about someone – their names, their abilities and what they look like. But to know them as a friend is different. You must talk with each other and spend time together. To get to know someone better, you do things together and share experiences.

Read aloud Philippians 3:10 – 4:1

If your group members have English as a second language, encourage them to read the passage a second time in their own language. This will help them to better understand the passage but it will also help them if and when they return home—see page 32.

There is a list of Bible words from this week's passage (NIV) on pages 26-27 of the Bible study booklet. Depending on your group, it may be appropriate to go through some or all of these words at this point. The word list for this study is shown over the page.

Leader's checklist

Have you...

- [ ] Reminded people of the time and place where you will meet? (By phone, email or text.)
- [ ] Prepared food and drinks?
- [ ] Sufficient Bibles or printed out sheets with the Bible passages on them?
- [ ] The optional Discipleship Explored DVD ready to play?
- [ ] Printed out the daily study material (if you are going to use it)?
- [ ] Thought through your answers to each of the questions?
- [ ] Prayed for each group member and yourself as the leader?

Bible words

v11 attain to the resurrection. To rise to life after I die.

v12 press on. Keep going.

v13 straining. Working hard to keep going.

v15 mature. Grown up.

v16 live up to. Live in a way that shows.

v16 attained. Achieved, gained.

v17 live according to the pattern we gave you. Live in the way we showed or taught you.

v19 their destiny. Their future after death.

v19 their glory is in their shame. They are proud of the sinful things that they do.

v20 citizenship. Home.

v20 eagerly await. Keenly wait for.

v21 transform. Completely change.

v21 lowly. Nothing special.

21 glorious. Wonderful.

4v1 stand firm in the Lord. Don't let anything take you away from the Lord.

Read Philippians 3:10-14

1 ***Are you surprised that Paul says that he wants to know Christ? Why?***

Paul had been a Christian for a long time, and was a leader and an apostle. We might think that he already knew everything there is to know about Jesus. Paul knows that he does not. What he means is that he wants to know Christ better. More deeply. More intimately.

This is the difference between knowing about Jesus and knowing Him as our Lord, Saviour and friend. If you are a Christian, you can say (verse 8) "I know Christ." But we also say: "I want to know Christ more and more."

Knowing Christ is much more than just knowing about him. Paul has already said that Christians are "in Christ" (see 1:1), and "united with Christ" (2:1).

2 ***How does Paul describe the cost of knowing Christ (verses 10-11)?***

"The fellowship of sharing in his suffering" and "becoming like him in death".

Follow-up question

What does Paul means by "the fellowship of sharing in his suffering"?
Suffering for Christ somehow helps us to know Christ better. It is a normal part of the Christian life.

Jesus promises that those who follow him will be persecuted (Mark 8:34-35). He also promises that God will bless those are persecuted for his sake (Matthew 5:11-12). This is part of the "cost" of being a Christian. When we choose Christ, we choose to live in opposition to the way the rest of the world lives. This will bring us into conflict.

Paul is not referring here to the kind of suffering that everyone goes through – illness, bereavement, unemployment etc, although God does use all of these things to change us on the inside and help us become more like Christ. Paul is referring to the suffering that is a normal part of every Christian's life, and which happens because we are disciples of Jesus. For example:

- Being rejected, laughed at or abused by family or friends because we are Christians.
- Losing your job because you won't give up Christ's standards.
- Being physically attacked by those who hate the gospel.

If you are "in Christ", suffering will be a part of your life, because it was part of Jesus' life. If we accept and even welcome suffering for Christ, then it becomes a way of knowing Christ better.

 *Follow-up question*

What does Paul means by "becoming like him in death"?

Refer the group back to Philippians 2:6-11. Jesus humbled himself, he was obedient to God, he came to serve others and die for them. We should be showing the same loving attitude and character Jesus shows.

(3) *What comforts come from knowing Christ (verses 10-11)?*

"The power of his resurrection" and "the resurrection from the dead".

 *Follow-up question*

What does Paul means by these two phrases?

- **The power of his resurrection:** This is the power of God, which brought Jesus back to life, and which is now at work in everyone who trusts in Jesus. It is God at work in us to make us alive spiritually and to strengthen us to serve him. I know Christ better, when I rely on his power to live for him and serve others. If I rely only on myself, I am missing out on knowing Christ better.
- **The resurrection from the dead:** This means eternal life beyond the grave. Christians believe that those who have a right relationship with Christ now will have an eternal relationship with him. God will clothe us in a new body to live with him in the new creation.

Ⓓ **Read Philippians 3 verse 12-16**

④ ***What is the "one thing" that Paul does (verses 12-14)?***

He presses on towards the goal of heaven (= the resurrection, eternal life with Christ).

❓ *Follow-up question*

How does Paul press on?

- Forget what is behind: Our old life is gone. We are made new in Christ, and now live a different way. We only look back if it helps us move forward...
- Strain towards what is ahead: We have to make an effort to live our lives for Jesus. The language suggests that this will involve hard work and self discipline.

❓ *Follow-up question*

Why does Paul do this?

To win the prize. Explain that Paul is using a sporting picture of athletes running a race. They do not get distracted by looking back. They look at the finishing line and head for it so that they can win the prize.

The Christian life is like the London Marathon. Everyone who crosses the finishing line wins a medal. It is not a short dash, but a long endurance race.

⑤ ***Do you think a Christian can ever be perfect?***

No – not yet! Christians will never stop being learners – disciples – in this life. God will make us perfect when he gives us a new body in the resurrection (verse 21).

It's important for new believers to understand this, so that they will not be tempted by false teachers who say that they can or should be perfect. It is also important so that they do not have the wrong ideas about Christian leaders (including you as their group leader!).

⑥ ***So what does it mean to be a "mature believer" (verse 15)?***

To know that we aren't perfect, but are pressing on to grow and know Christ better.

Read Philippians 3:17 – 4:1

7 ***Paul says there are only two ways to live. What are they?***

Verse 18: Enemies of the cross of Christ.

Verses 17 and 20: Living according to the pattern Paul gave – i.e. genuine disciples. Living as citizens of heaven, waiting keenly for Jesus to return.

8 ***Where do these two ways lead?***

Heaven and hell.

Follow-up question

How should we feel about the fact that some people are going to hell?
Paul responds with tears (verse 18). We could easily take joy in the fact that those who persecute us will be punished, but this is not right. Jesus said we must love our enemies and pray for those who persecute us (Matthew 5:44). We must continue to "shine like stars as we hold out the word of life" to them (2:15-16).

9 ***What does it mean to be a citizen of heaven?***

Encourage any internationals in your group to think what it means to be a citizen of their home country living in a foreign land. They are ambassadors or representatives, who show other people what it is like to be a citizen of their home country. We live by the rules and standards of the country we belong to. If we are citizens of heaven, we should be showing people what heaven is like by the way we live. Heaven is our home, so we should live by heaven's standards.

10 ***Paul says that our "citizenship is in heaven" and that Christ will return? How will these facts help us to press on?***

We have already seen that it is normal for a Christian to suffer because of their faith in Jesus. For some, this suffering may be severe, long-term or even lead to death. But everyone who is a follower of Jesus knows that life on this earth is only temporary. We are already citizens of heaven and have a right relationship with God through Christ. We can look forward to living with Christ forever, with a new body (verse 21) and enjoying the new creation – a new heaven and new earth. As Paul has already said: "to live is Christ and to die is gain" (1:21).

If you have internationals in your group, this question will be especially important for them, particularly if they are likely to face opposition or persecution when they return home. Help them to see that it is normal for a Christian to suffer because of their faith in Jesus. This does not mean that God has deserted them. No matter how difficult things become, we can be certain that we have a sure future to look forward to, with Jesus forever.

11 ***From Philippians chapter 3 can you summarise how we can "stand firm in the Lord" (4:1)?***

Note: *This question will help you to check how well the group have understood this session's teaching. But don't expect them to come up with all of the following answers! Depending on your group, you may want to mention the following verses to help your group write their summary.*

- Rejoice in the Lord (3:1)
- Put no confidence in the flesh (3:3)
- Want to know Christ better and better (3:10)
- Forget what is behind (3:13)
- Press on as a disciple of Jesus (3:12, 14)
- Follow Paul's example and others who live according to the pattern he gave (3:17) – such as Timothy (2:19-24) and Epaphroditus (2:25-30)
- Look forward to Christ's return from heaven (3:20).

MEMORY VERSE

"I want to know Christ and the power of his resurrection and the fellowship of sharing in his sufferings." Philippians 3:10. At the end of each session we have included a memory verse taken from the Bible passage the group has studied. You may find it helpful to read this together as you finish the session. Ask your group members to learn this verse during the week. If your group members have English as a second language, encourage them to learn the verse in their own language as well.

PRAY

- Thank God that you have been saved by Christ and so you can eagerly wait for his return.
- Ask God to help you to press on as a disciple of Jesus.
- Pray for any you know whose "destiny is destruction" (3:19).
- Ask God to help you to stand firm in the Lord.

DVD

If you feel it's appropriate for your group, you may want to show the *Discipleship Explored* DVD at this point. The DVD can be used as a summary or as a refresher for the main teaching point in this session.

DAILY BIBLE STUDIES

We have prepared some simple daily Bible-reading notes for you to use with the group, which reinforce some of the truths that have been learned at this session, and encourage them to start a daily discipline of Bible reading and prayer. The notes are available for download from www.discipleshipexplored.org

Group members will benefit from the model of having a daily time with God. But use these notes with discretion – they may be too much for some to attempt.

CONCLUSION

Finish by encouraging your group members to come back next week. Tell them: "You might have got the impression with what we've looked at so far that being a disciple is a bit grim. Next week we'll see how it is exactly the opposite."

Additional notes for leaders

What does it mean to know Christ? This is a wonderful mystery. I live in Christ. He lives in me. Knowing Christ better is about experiencing his life as it flows more and more through our life now. This is explained in the three phrases Paul uses to describe what it means to know Christ in verses 10-11: "the power of his resurrection", "the fellowship of sharing in his sufferings" and "becoming like him in death". Being a disciple is a lifelong process of getting to know Christ better. We will never know Christ fully in this world, so we will always need to grow in our faith and understanding. See 1 Corinthians 13:12.

Why does Paul say "somehow" in verse 11? This is not Paul saying that he has doubts or is uncertain that he will be raised from the dead. He means that the exact way God will do this is unclear to him. It is a wonderful mystery. (See 1 Corinthians 15:51.)

Why does Paul link "the power of his resurrection", "the fellowship of sharing in his sufferings" and "becoming like him in death" with knowing Christ? We tend to think that suffering and death are bad, resurrection and life are good. But Paul thinks that all these experiences are good because they help us to know Christ better – which is the greatest thing of all (3:8).

Will all mature Christians believe exactly the same things? **Yes** – on the important points of the gospel, mature believers will be certain – that it is through faith in Jesus alone that we are saved. **No** – there will always be matters of church tradition and opinion where mature believers will have differing ideas. Encourage young Christians that they should not be troubled when they meet Christians who have different ideas, so long as they are firm on the basics.

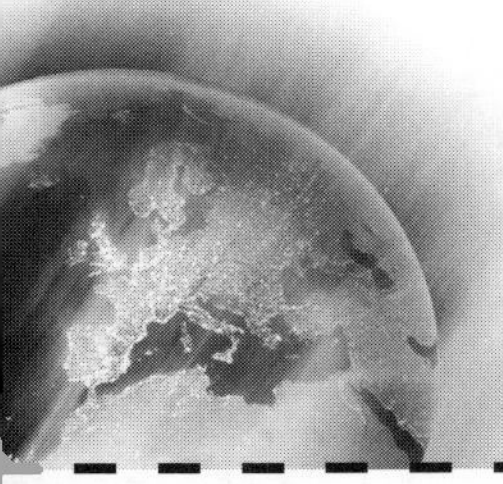

WEEK 7: PHILIPPIANS 4:2-9

How can I rejoice in Christ?

RECAP

Recap what we learned last week or ask the group to summarise what they learned last week. If needed, there is a short summary on page 29 of the Bible study booklet.

OPENING DISCUSSION QUESTION

What things make you worry? What do you do when you are anxious?

Make sure that this discussion does not take over the whole session! People can talk for hours about their problems. Listen carefully to the answers to this question. It will help you understand the kind of difficulties people in your group are facing. It will help you know how to pray for them. And there will be some practical things you can do to help. If needed, arrange for you or your co-leader to meet with people or talk with them later about any problems they are especially worried about.

Explain to the group that we will be looking later in this session at how Christians should deal with their worries.

Read aloud Philippians 4:2-9

If your group members have English as a second language, encourage them to read the passage a second time in their own language. This will help them to better understand the passage but it will also help them if and when they return home—see page 32.

There is a list of Bible words from this week's passage (NIV) on pages 30-31 of the Bible study booklet. Depending on your group, it may be appropriate to go through some or all of these words at this point. The word list for this study is shown over the page.

Leader's checklist

Have you...

- [ ] Reminded people of the time and place where you will meet? (By phone, email or text.)
- [ ] Prepared food and drinks?
- [ ] Sufficient Bibles or printed out sheets with the Bible passages on them?
- [ ] The optional Discipleship Explored DVD ready to play?
- [ ] Printed out the daily study material (if you are going to use it)?
- [ ] Thought through your answers to each of the questions?
- [ ] Prayed for each group member and yourself as the leader?

Bible words

v2 plead. Ask for something that you want very much.

v3 loyal yokefellow. True friend.

v3 contended. Worked hard, struggled.

v3 in the cause of the gospel. For the gospel.

v3 the book of life. A picture used in the Bible to talk about the list of people who God has chosen and saved through Jesus Christ.

v4 rejoice in. Find joy in, take delight in.

v5 evident to all. Seen by everyone.

v6 anxious. Worried.

v6 petition. Humbly asking for something.

v6 your requests. What you are asking for.

v7 transcends. Is far beyond.

v7 guard. Keep safe.

v8 noble. Good.

v8 admirable. Something you should admire (respect).

v9 put it into practice. Do it.

Read Philippians 4:2-3

(1) *What encouraging things do verses 2-3 tell us about the two women Euodia and Syntyche?*

- They are both Christians.
- They contended at Paul's side – they worked with Paul to tell others the gospel (see 1:27).
- Paul considered them to be his "fellow workers".
- Their names are in "the book of life". Explain that this phrase means that they are Christians, and that because they have put their faith in Jesus, they can be certain of having eternal life (see Revelation 20:15; 21:27).

Paul doesn't get involved in the detail of the disagreement between these two women. Instead he tells them that they must "agree with each other in the Lord" (verse 2).

Note: *Their disagreement cannot have been about false teaching which threatened the gospel. If it had been, we can be sure that Paul would have corrected that false teaching just as he had done in chapter 3.*

(2) *What do you think it means to agree in the Lord?*

We must remember that we are united in Christ, have the same heavenly Father, and should have the same purpose – to know Christ and to make him known. We may disagree on the precise way to understand some parts of the Bible, or on how we do things as Christians, but must not let these things ruin our unity on the important things. It is understandable that Christians will disagree with each other in all kinds of things, but we must agree about the thing that unites us – Christ and the gospel.

- ***How can we help each other do that (like the "loyal yokefellow" in verse 3)?***

- Paul did not take sides – we shouldn't either. Instead we should aim to help those who disagree to be reconciled.
- We should remind each other of the things that unite us: who Jesus is, why he came and our responsibility to tell others about him.
- See also 2:1-4: we must have the same love, be one in spirit and purpose, and do nothing out of selfish ambition. There may be things that we need to repent of in our disagreements.

Optional follow-up question

- ***Why was Paul anxious that the women agree with each other? (See 2:3-5 & 1:27.)***
- In 2:3-5 Paul has already said that Christians are to "consider others better than yourselves" and that their "attitude is to be the same as that of Christ Jesus". Both women need to be prepared to adopt the attitude of Jesus – taking the initiative, making themselves humble, serving others – even if such actions come at a great personal cost.
- In 1:27 Paul says: "Conduct yourselves in a manner worthy of the gospel of Christ". In this way they will "stand firm in one spirit, contending as one man for the faith of the gospel".
- If these women are going to show the same attitude as Christ, they need to agree in the Lord. If they don't, their conduct will have an impact on how they and the rest of the Philippian Christians share the gospel with unbelievers.

Read Philippians 4:4-7

3. ***Paul tells us to "rejoice in the Lord always". Do you think this is possible? Why or why not?***

Yes, because it is the Lord we rejoice in, not our circumstances.

We can rejoice as we remember his promises (Jesus will return; we will know him completely; we too will be resurrected on the last day; the Lord is near and so on).

(4) *What should we do as Christians when we are feeling worried?*

- We should rejoice in the Lord.
- We should pray about it.
- We should give thanks.

(5) *How do these things help us not to be anxious?*

Rejoicing, praying and giving thanks are not about pretending everything is OK when it is not. Paul is not saying "rejoice in your circumstances" or "rejoice in the pain you feel". He says that we are to "rejoice in the Lord". We are to remember that God is good whatever has happened to us. He has not changed.

- He is our loving father who has saved us through Christ.
- He always listens to our prayers.
- He is patient and gentle with us.
- He always keeps his promises.
- He is in control of everything, and will make sure he finishes the good work he started in us.

Praying about our worries helps us to trust God whatever the situation. We can give our concerns to God, who cares for us and will do what is right and good for us and for his kingdom.

Being thankful will help us think more clearly about everything we have in Christ, rather than being upset about the things we do not have.

"I have yet to meet a chronic worrier who enjoys an excellent prayer life." Don Carson, *Basics for believers*.

(6) *What will be the result if we obey verses 4-6? (See verse 7.)*

God's peace will guard our hearts and minds. It guards our hearts so that we continue to love God and want the things he wants, rather than other things. It guards our minds so that we remain true to the gospel, rather than chase after other things.

Read Philippians 4 verse 8-9

7 ***What should we spend our time thinking about?***

Check that your group understands the meaning of these words:

- Whatever is true.
- Whatever is noble. i.e. good.
- Whatever is right.
- Whatever is pure. i.e. not tainted by false motives.
- Whatever is lovely. i.e. it has a beauty that comes from God.
- Whatever is admirable. i.e. something you should admire or respect.
- Whatever is excellent or praiseworthy.

Notice that all these things are true of Jesus Christ.

It is not just "Christian" things that we think about – "whatever" includes anything in the world that exhibits these qualities. Whenever friendships, music, literature, hobbies, family, art, sport, nature etc display these qualities, we can enjoy them and give thanks that their goodness comes from God.

8 ***Write down the opposites of the words that Paul uses in verse 8. How would you be different if you spent time thinking about these things?***

Whatever is false... dishonest... wrong... polluted... ugly... shameful... shoddy or deserving condemnation.

- If we constantly think about things like these, they will become normal to us, and they will seem like an acceptable way to behave.
- It will discourage us from living like Christ.
- We will no longer "shine like stars" – being different from those around us. We will become like them.
- It will stop us rejoicing in the Lord, and make us glory in our shame (3:19).

Our minds are filled with the things we watch, read, do and listen to: TV, internet sites, magazines, books, computer games, books and music.

9 So how can we encourage each other to fill our minds with things that are noble, right, pure, etc.? Give practical answers.

Remember that these things apply to what we do with others as well as what we do on our own.

- We should be honest with each other about what we are reading, seeing and doing.
- Admit the things we are struggling with.
- Have friends we are accountable to and who will ask questions about what we are reading or watching.
- We need to avoid getting involved in unhelpful conversations, where people are gossiping or being cruel to others.
- When we watch TV or movies, ask ourselves: "Would I be embarrassed to watch this with more mature Christian friends?"
- Talk about the good things we have seen, read or heard, and recommend them to each other.
- Be prepared to gently challenge each other.
- Learn from the example of more mature Christians (verse 9).
- Ask God to help us do all these things – we cannot do them on our own.

Note: *Be aware that as we aim to think and behave in a godly way, we will be brought into conflict with our non-Christian friends and family. Many church fellowships also settle for lower standards than they should. This will be a struggle for many new Christians.*

10 What is the command in verse 9 and what is promised?

- **Command:** put into practice – what you have learned or received or heard (from Paul) or seen (in Paul).
- **Promise:** the God of peace will be with you.

In verses 4-9, Paul has told us to agree in the Lord, rejoice in the Lord, pray to the Lord, and think in a way that pleases the Lord.

11 ***What will you find most difficult about doing what Paul tells us?***

Encourage your group to give specific answers. If they find this hard, ask them to think of an example in the coming week when they might find it difficult to agree in the Lord, rejoice in the Lord etc.

MEMORY VERSE

***"Do not be anxious about anything, but in everything, by prayer and petition, with thanksgiving, present your requests to God."* Philippians 4:6.**

At the end of each session we have included a memory verse taken from the Bible passage the group has studied. You may find it helpful to read this together as you finish the session. Ask your group members to learn this verse during the week. If your group members have English as a second language, encourage them to learn the verse in their own language as well.

PRAY

Use the group's answers to question 11 as the basis for your prayers for each other.

DVD

If you feel it's appropriate for your group, you may want to show the *Discipleship Explored* DVD at this point. The DVD can be used as a summary or as a refresher for the main teaching point in this session.

DAILY BIBLE STUDIES

We have prepared some simple daily Bible-reading notes for you to use with the group, which reinforce some of the truths that have been learned at this session, and encourage them to start a daily discipline of Bible reading and prayer. The notes are available for download from www.discipleshipexplored.org

Group members will benefit from the model of having a daily time with God. But use these notes with discretion – they may be too much for some to attempt.

CONCLUSION

Finish by encouraging your group members to come back next week. Tell them: "I hope you've seen from this week that being a disciple should be full of joy at what Christ has done for us, and is doing in us. Next week, we'll discover one of the most important secrets about living the Christian life."

Additional notes for leaders

What is "the peace of God, which transcends all understanding"? People often read this verse and think that God will give them a feeling of peace. This may be true for some. But it is important to help young Christians understand the role of feelings, and to protect them from putting their trust in feelings rather than the facts. Our feelings may change. The facts of the gospel do not.

- Christians already have peace with God – the peace he has created between us and him through Jesus (Romans 5:1). We were at war because of our sin. Now we are at peace because Jesus has taken the punishment for our sin.
- The fact that we are at peace with God means that we no longer need to be anxious. We can have "feelings of peace" because this peace truly exists.
- The peace we have with God is so wonderful that no one can fully understand or explain it.
- God's peace guards us.

"Transcends" can have a double meaning here. It can mean "beyond" in the sense of "we can't understand it". But it can also mean "better than" in the sense of "it is better than knowing all the answers". There is much we don't know but having peace with God, and so being able to trust him totally, is better than knowing all the answers now.

What does Paul mean when he says "the God of peace will be with you"? The promise of verse 9 is plural – "The God of peace will be with you **all**."

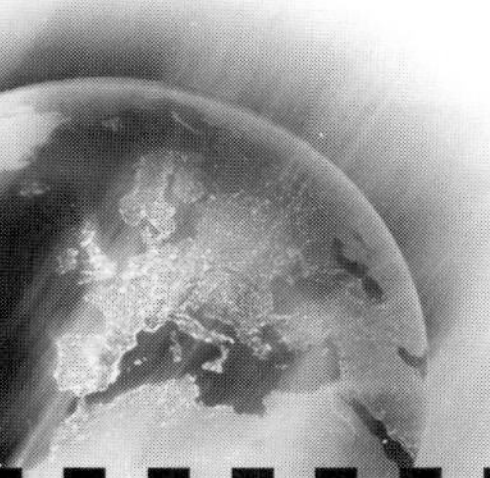

WEEK 8: PHILIPPIANS 4:10-23

How can I be content in Christ?

RECAP

Recap what we learned last week or ask the group to summarise what they learned last week. If needed, there is a short summary on page 33 of the Bible study booklet.

OPENING DISCUSSION QUESTION

"My life would be great if only…"
How would people you know answer that question?
How would you answer it?

People in general believe that contentment is about having more stuff, being in different circumstances, having better relationships, having more money. Try to get people to talk about all of these areas.

Optional follow-up question

- ***Why do they think people today are so often discontent?***

Read aloud Philippians 4:10-23

If your group members have English as a second language, encourage them to read the passage a second time in their own language. This will help them to better understand the passage but it will also help them if and when they return home—see page 32.

There is a list of Bible words from this week's passage (NIV) on pages 34-35 of the Bible study booklet. Depending on your group, it may be appropriate to go through some or all of these words at this point. The word list for this study is shown over the page.

Leader's checklist

Have you…

- ☐ Thought about what to suggest next for people finishing the course?
- ☐ Prepared food and drinks?
- ☐ Sufficient Bibles or printed out sheets with the Bible passages on them?
- ☐ The optional Discipleship Explored DVD ready to play?
- ☐ Printed out the daily study material (if you are going to use it)?
- ☐ Thought through your answers to each of the questions?
- ☐ Prayed for each group member and yourself as the leader?

Bible words

v10 renewed. Started again.

v10 concern. Take an interest in.

v11 I am in need. I don't have the things that I need.

v11 content. Satisfied.

v11 circumstances. Situation.

v12 to have plenty. To have even more than I need.

v12 in want. Poor.

v15 moreover. Also.

v15 in the early days. Near the beginning.

v15 acquaintance with the gospel. Personal knowledge of the gospel.

v15 set out. Left.

v15 Macedonia. Philippi was in Macedonia, part of ancient Greece.

v15 shared with. Involved with, helped.

v15 Thessalonica. Another city in Macedonia.

v16 aid. Help.

v17 credited. Added.

v18 I am amply supplied. I have everything I need.

v18 fragrant. Sweet smelling, pleasing.

v18 acceptable sacrifice. A gift to God that pleases him.

v19 according to. In proportion to.

v19 glorious. Wonderful.

v22 Caesar's household. The people who live and work in Caesar's house.

v22 Amen. A Hebrew word which means "certainly" or "so be it".

Read Philippians 4:10-13

Paul wrote this letter from prison. We know from the rest of the Bible that Paul had known times of comfort and times of great trouble.

1. ***What situations does Paul list in verse 12?***

- Well fed
- Hungry
- In plenty
- In want

Optional follow-up question

• Read 2 Corinthians 11:24-28. What difficult situations did Paul face?
Paul was a Roman citizen, had an education and was most likely from a privileged family. And yet he experienced great pain, danger, hard work, lack of sleep, hunger, thirst and being cold and naked – as well as his daily concerns for Christians. He faced all of these situations because of his faith in Christ and his determination to tell others the gospel message.

2 *Why do you think it is important to be content whether we are rich or poor?*

"Living in plenty is as miserable as living in poverty if you haven't learned the secret of contentment." (Discipleship Explored DVD)

There are many people who are wealthy but discontent. Money does not always make people happy! And poverty does not always make people sad. There are many people who are financially poor but very happy.

Christians may be rich or poor. God does not promise to make us rich but he does promise to help us to be content no matter what situation we are in.

Wealth can distract us from the important thing in life – knowing Christ and making him known. Poverty can do the same. Jesus says that riches and the desire for things can choke out the word of God in our lives (Mark 4:19).

3 *What is the secret of being content?*

Verse 13: We can only be content with God's help – we cannot do it on our own. We need to trust God to help us.

4 *How can we learn to be content in our circumstances?*

We are often discontent because we forget what we have in Christ. Emphasize that we need to learn to be content – to train ourselves not to focus on our own feelings of discontent but on the facts of the gospel, and the new priorities of our lives as Jesus' disciples.

Follow-up question

- ***Where did Paul find contentment?***
- **In knowing Christ** – this was the most precious thing in the world to Paul. The things we own are nothing compared with the riches of knowing Christ.
- **In making the gospel known to others** – any kind of hardship is possible to live with if people are hearing the gospel which can save them.

5 *Does verse 13 mean that Paul has a super-human ability to do anything? If not, what does he mean?*

No! We need to read this verse as part of Paul's explanation of the secret of being content. He has learned that God will give him the strength he needs to be content in any circumstance.

The same is true for us. This verse does not mean that we can walk on water or fly through the air if we believe enough! But like Paul, we can trust God to give us the strength we need to be content in any situation.

Read Philippians 4:14-19

Although Paul is content in prison, he is also grateful for the gift the Philippian Christians sent to him.

6 ***How does Paul describe their giving in verses 14 and 18?***

- They shared in his troubles (verse 14). ***What does this mean?*** They weren't just sending money. Paul knew that they cared for him, were praying for him, and knew what he was going through. Giving is encouraging!
- Their gifts were a sweet-smelling offering to God, and an acceptable sacrifice which was pleasing to God. God is pleased by generous giving.

Their giving came out of their partnership in the gospel with Paul. They sent Epaphroditus to help him (2:25), as well as gifts to meet his needs. We are not told precisely what this was – it no doubt included money, but may also have been food, books, clothes etc.

7 ***What is the pattern of giving that we see in these verses and how can we follow it? (See also verses 10-11.)***

- Verses 10 & 14: They were concerned for Paul and wanted to encourage and help him. Give in a way that encourages the person you are giving to. E.g. along with the gift send a letter, assure them of your prayers or even send someone to visit.
- Verse 15: They gave even when others did not. Give even if others are not giving.
- Verse 15: They gave as a church. Give as a fellowship. There may also be a place for an individual to support another, but the pattern here is that the church as a whole gave to Paul and supported him.
- Verse 16: They kept giving to support Paul, through the good times and bad times. Go on giving. Supporting gospel work is not a one-time thing. Regular planned giving is important.
- Verse 16: They gave as generously as they were able. Be generous givers.
- Verse 18: Their gifts to Paul were gifts to God. Give to God. Even though your giving is supporting people in gospel work, we need to remember that when we give, God is pleased with us. We are giving to his work.

8 ***Read verse 19. Does this mean that Christians will never be poor? Why or why not?***

Yes! But we are not talking about money! Christians will always be rich, because we are rich in Christ.

The promise is that God will meet our *needs,* not our *wants*. We can trust him to supply us with everything we need. This may or may not include earthly wealth. God knows what we need, and knows what is best for us – and He will give it to us. God may allow us to be persecuted, made homeless, or lose our job or health. We need to trust that what we receive from him is good for us and the gospel.

Read Philippians 4 verse 20-23

Although Paul is content in prison, he is also grateful for the gift the Philippian Christians sent to him.

9 What is so encouraging about the way Paul ends his letter – especially verse 22?

- He gives God the glory for everything.
- It is personal – it shows he loves them as his own family.
- He sends greetings to them from the other believers with him.
- He says that there are some in Caesar's household who have become Christians (from 1:13 we only knew that they had heard the gospel).
- He prays for them.

10 Tell the rest of the group one thing that has helped you grow as a disciple as you have studied Philippians together.

This question is to help the group express how they have grown. Encourage them to look back over the letter.

Optional follow-up question

- ***If you think your group is able, ask them to work together to come up with a simple sentence to sum up what a disciple is.***

From Philippians they could come up with something like this:
"A disciple is someone who has been saved by Christ, and who is growing with other believers to know Christ better and make him known."

MEMORY VERSE

"I have learned the secret of being content in any and every situation." Philippians 4:12. At the end of each session we have included a memory verse taken from the Bible passage the group has studied. You may find it helpful to read this together as you finish the session. Ask your group members to learn this verse during the week. If your group members have English as a second language, encourage them to learn the verse in their own language as well.

PRAY

- Ask God to help you to learn the secret of being content in every situation.
- Pray about your giving.
- Give thanks for things that people have said have helped them to grow as disciples.

DVD

If you feel it's appropriate for your group, you may want to show the *Discipleship Explored* DVD at this point. The DVD can be used as a summary or as a refresher for the main teaching point in this session.

DAILY BIBLE STUDIES

We have prepared some simple daily Bible-reading notes for you to use with the group, which reinforce some of the truths that have been learned at this session, and encourage them to start a daily discipline of Bible reading and prayer. The notes are available for download from www.discipleshipexplored.org

Group members will benefit from the model of having a daily time with God. But use these notes with discretion – they may be too much for some to attempt.

WHAT NEXT?

What will happen to the members of your group now that you have finished these studies? You may want to build in some time during this final study to discuss possible options for the future:

- Could you continue to meet as a group, perhaps studying together the book of Acts, an Old Testament book or overview, or another of Paul's letters?
- Is there another group or course available that members can join?
- Could you provide Bible-reading material for each group member, so that they can continue to read God's word at home?
- How can you help each other to "stand firm in the Lord"?

If it would suit your group members, you may like to give them a feedback form. An example feedback form can be downloaded from www.discipleshipexplored.org

If your group includes members from other cultures, see also the section on "Cross-cultural Discipleship" on page 29 of this book.

CONCLUSION

Thank your group members for being part of this group. Encourage them to keep praying for each other and helping each other to live for Christ. Encourage them to go out and be Christ's disciples in the world: filled with joy and truth; eager to tell others about Christ; humble and godly; shining like stars; supporting and helping each other.

Additional notes for leaders

How can we learn to be content whatever the circumstances? Paul has already told the Philippian Christians plenty of things that will help them to be content in all situations:

- God will finish the work he started in us. We can be sure that God will not fail us. A Christian can feel secure and confident in God, and so should not need to search for other things to give them these feelings.
- We can be confident that God loves us because Jesus Christ died for us. That is what gives Christians their sense of significance – not our worldly status or wealth.
- "For me to live is Christ and to die is gain" (1:21). There is nothing that can harm me in this world. The worst that can happen – death – will only bring me closer to Christ.
- Our citizenship is in heaven. We have a secure future in Christ, and will enjoy him forever. This means we do not need to reach for wealth, experiences and possessions in this world.
- God is in charge of our circumstances. He has put us where we are so that we can be his person – his disciple – in that situation.

What does Paul mean by "I am looking for what may be credited to your account" (verse17)? Paul is saying that he wants the Philippian Christians to have the blessing (the good things from God) that comes from giving to others.

What should be our priorities in giving? Give for gospel work. Our giving should mainly support the work of the gospel, because that is the most important thing (1:18). Giving to poverty, famine or disaster relief should not be neglected, but our priority must always be to support those who are working to make Christ known.

EXTRA: PHILIPPIANS 2:19-30

An *example* to follow?

This session is deliberately short!

You might use it half-way through the course, between weeks 4 and 5, or you could use it at the end. You might want to think about how you can use this differently in order to give some variation to your meetings. You could, for example:

- *Have a shorter Bible study time, after a longer time of general talk over a meal.*
- *Invite some other Christians to share their testimonies or experiences for the encouragement of the group.*
- *Have an extended prayer time.*
- *Invite members of the group to share their own testimonies, or tell the group how they have been growing since they became a Christian.*

Or alternatively, if you don't have room for 9 meetings, you could encourage the group to use this session as a home study for themselves, and discuss any issues that arise at the start of the next study.

Please note there is no DVD talk that links with this Bible study.

Leader's checklist

Have you...

- [ ] Reminded people of the time and place where you will meet? (By phone, email or text.)
- [ ] Prepared food and drinks?
- [ ] Sufficient Bibles or printed out sheets with the Bible passages on them?
- [ ] The optional Discipleship Explored DVD ready to play?
- [ ] Printed out the daily study material (if you are going to use it)?
- [ ] Thought through your answers to each of the questions?
- [ ] Prayed for each group member and yourself as the leader?

OPENING DISCUSSION QUESTION

Who did you want to be like when you were a child? Why was that person, or their job, attractive to you?

This can be a light-hearted discussion. It is just intended to introduce the theme of role-models, before starting the study.

Read aloud Philippians 2:19-30

If your group members have English as a second language,

encourage them to read the passage a second time in their own language. This will help them to better understand the passage but it will also help them if and when they return home—see page 32.

There is a list of Bible words from this week's passage (NIV) on page 37 of the Bible study booklet. Depending on your group, it may be appropriate to go through some or all of these words at this point. The word list for this study is shown below.

Bible words

v19 be cheered. Be made happy.

v20 takes a genuine interest in your welfare. Truly cares about how well you are doing.

v21 looks out for. Is interested in.

v22 proved himself. Shown that he is good.

v26 distressed. Very sad and worried.

v27 to spare me sorrow upon sorrow. To keep me from lots of sadness.

v28 I am … eager. I want very much.

v30 risking his life. He was in danger of dying.

Read Philippians 2:19-24

Paul longs to visit the Philippian Christians again, to see for himself how they are getting on. But he is in prison, so he is hoping to send two of his friends, Timothy and Epaphroditus, to them.

1 What do we learn about Timothy and what matters to him from these verses?

- He truly cares for them (verse 20). Notice that this is practical love – he is interested in their welfare.
- He is an evangelist (verse 22) – he wants to spread the good news.
- He works with Paul (verse 22) – he works in a team, not on his own.
- He is committed to Jesus (verse 21) – he is not living for himself, but for Jesus.

2 What kind of relationship does Paul have with Timothy?

- Paul has no one else like Timothy (verse 20). This combination of a Christian worker who is willing to serve and has a genuine love for others is quite rare!
- Paul thinks of Timothy as a son (verse 22). As part of the Christian family, we can enjoy close relationships with others.

Read Philippians 2:25-30 and 4:18

3 ***Who was Epaphroditus and what happened to him?***

- Epaphroditus was sent from Philippi to take news to Paul, and to help look after him in prison (verses 2:25, 30; 4:18).
- He became very ill and almost died (verses 26-27, 30)
- He wanted to go back home (verse 26).

Notice that Paul is neither angry with him, nor disappointed with him. Epaphroditus isn't a failure for getting ill, or then 'being homesick' for his brothers and sisters in Christ.

Note: *Just because we are working for the Lord, it does not mean that we will not suffer problems and difficulties, or that plans we have made for good reasons will not go wrong.*

4 ***Why do you think Paul encourages the Philippian Christians to welcome Epaphroditus back?***

- Epaphroditus deserves their honour and respect because he has risked everything for Christ.
- Epaphroditus may also be feeling guilty and think he has failed.
- The Philippian Christians may think he has failed!
- His return actually helps Paul to be less anxious (verse 28).

5 ***In what three ways does Paul describe Epaphroditus in verse 25? What do they teach us about the Christian life?***

- Brother: We are all one in Christ Jesus. Paul, the great apostle, is a brother to the humble messenger Epaphroditus.
- Fellow-worker: We serve Jesus together – there are no higher and lower Christians. We work as a team, not as individuals.
- Fellow soldier: It is a fight! It will be hard work, stressful and difficult. We should not expect it to be easy.

(6) *Timothy and Epaphroditus are both young Christians, but Paul still uses them as examples to follow. How can we be examples to others?*

Recap the qualities of the two:

- Serving Jesus – not living for themselves
- Serving humbly alongside others
- Hard work
- Dependable
- Willing to do anything for the gospel.

Note that these qualities do not depend on how old someone is or how long they have been a Christian. The question is whether we are living as disciples, following Jesus wholeheartedly and wanting to put Jesus at the centre of everything we do. We can all be examples to others.

PRAY

Thank God for the examples of Paul, Timothy and Epaphroditus. Pray for each other and ask God to help you to be examples to others.

DVD

There is no DVD talk that links with this session.

DAILY BIBLE STUDIES

We have prepared some simple daily Bible-reading notes for you to use with the group, which reinforce some of the truths that have been learned at this session, and encourage them to start a daily discipline of Bible reading and prayer. The notes are available for download from www.discipleshipexplored.org

Group members will benefit from the model of having a daily time with God. But use these notes with discretion – they may be too much for some to attempt.

CONCLUSION

Finish by encouraging your group members to come back next week.